lantana

Anthony LaPaglia as Leon in *Lantana*. (Photo: Elise Lockwood.)

lantana

original screenplay
by **andrew bovell**
based on his play,
speaking in tongues

Currency Press, Sydney

CURRENCY SCREENPLAYS
General Editor: Nick Parsons

First published in 2001 by
Currency Press Pty Ltd
PO Box 2287
Strawberry Hills NSW 2012
www.currency.com.au
enquiries@currency.com.au

Second printing 2003

NATIONAL LIBRARY OF AUSTRALIA CIP DATA
Bovell, Andrew.
    Lantana.
    ISBN 0 86819 714 9
    I. Bovell, Andrew. Speaking in tongues. II. Title.
    A822.3

Cover design by Kate Florance; cover image by Vanessa White, courtesy of Jan Chapman Films.
Production stills within the text courtesy of Jan Chapman Films.
Printed by Bookmarque, Croydon, Surrey, UK

Contents

Anthony LaPaglia as Leon and Kerry Armstrong as Sonja in *Lantana*.
(Photo: Elise Lockwood.)

Writer's Note

Andrew Bovell

The screenplay published here is the culmination of a decade of work. It began in 1992 when the Melbourne theatre group Five Dollar Theatre Company commissioned me to write a short piece for a season of plays entitled *Suitcases in a Thousand Room Hotel*. The resulting piece *Like Whiskey on the Breath of a Drunk You Love* used various theatrical techniques such as split scenes and simultaneous dialogue. Although it was a fairly tongue-in-cheek take on the game of seduction and the pitfalls of marriage I could sense something of more substance laid at its core. The four characters—two married couples, Leon and Sonja, and Jane and Pete—shared an undefined yearning. I didn't attempt to make this explicit in the piece. I was happy to let it sit beneath the surface with the idea that somewhere down the track I would come back and explore it more deeply.

Later I was commissioned by another Melbourne theatre group, Chameleon, to write a short play for their season entitled *Tidal Wave*. *Distant Lights From Dark Places* as the piece was called was first performed at La Mama in Melbourne in 1994. It explores a chain of connection between four isolated figures, Valerie, Sarah, Nik and Neil. Although much darker in tone and a more sophisticated piece of writing than *Whiskey* it also used parallel narrative, split scenes and simultaneous dialogue.

Companies like Chameleon and Five Dollar formed the bedrock of theatre practice in Melbourne in the early 1990s. They provided an arena for writers, directors and performers to experiment with form. In both these early pieces I was experimenting with formal ideas that would take my writing beyond naturalism and better reveal the shape of human experience as I was observing it. I was able to consolidate these ideas through my association with Ros Horin and the Griffin Theatre Company in Sydney.

Ros had directed *Whiskey* in a season of short plays at the Stables in 1993. Sometime after that she approached me with the idea of a doing a season of *Whiskey* and *Distant Lights* and commissioning a third piece to accompany them. Instead of an anthology of three unconnected short plays I suggested to Ros that I write a full-length play that would bring the two short plays together. And so the idea of *Speaking in Tongues* was born.

At about the same time Mickey Camilleri approached me to write a treatment for a film. She was very open and supportive about what that film might be. It was then that I first began to explore the two short plays for material that might make a film. Simultaneously I was able to explore some further possibilities for the full-length play as well. Although in the end Mickey and I were unable to go beyond this initial treatment it laid the foundation for the film and I owe a debt of thanks to Mickey for her support at this time.

On the surface the two plays have little in common yet the characters in both plays share the same sense of yearning I had identified in the earlier piece. They are all searching for a sense of clarification in their emotional lives. I was able to go back to Leon and Sonja and Jane and Pete and follow their lives beyond the rigid parameters set down in the original piece. In effect I was able to explore the consequences of what had taken place in the original play.

Distant Lights remains virtually unchanged and forms the central piece of *Speaking in Tongues*. The challenge was to make the connection between the two pieces more explicit. Taking two characters from *Whiskey*, Leon and Jane, and making them witness crucial events that were played out or alluded to in *Distant Lights* achieved this. In bearing witness to events in the other play Leon and Jane were able to make further sense of their own lives whilst also allowing me to set up what was to come in the drama. From this point on the destinies of all eight characters were linked and this interconnection between disparate people emerged as a strong theme in the work.

For the third and final Act I took Leon from *Whiskey* and brought him into the world of *Distant Lights* by making him the policeman who was investigating Valerie's disappearance. Whilst in *Distant Lights* my interest had been in Valerie, exploring her story through a series a phone messages she leaves for her husband, in *Speaking in Tongues* I saw the opportunity to explore the story of the man who came home to those messages, and so I introduced her husband John. I distinctly remember the moment of discovering that this was not a story about a man who came home to find those messages at all but a story about a man who had been home all the time and had heard those messages but failed to act. This was not something I knew when I wrote *Distant Lights* but something discovered in the writing of *Speaking in Tongues*. It was a defining moment in the writing process and became the final revelation in the play. To me it says something about the moral weakness to which we are all susceptible simply by virtue of being human. That the consequences of such a weakness are so tragic epitomizes this story.

At the time of writing the play I was very interested in the notion that different points of view might glean quite different and sometimes contrary meaning from the same incident. I was interested in finding new narrative shapes in the theatre. I wanted to work on a lateral plain rather than a linear one. I was interested in the random connections between people and how we make sense of our own lives through encountering the lives of others. I was influenced by the multi-narrative films of Robert Altman, and later films such as *Happiness* (Todd Solondz) and *Magnolia* (Paul Thomas Anderson). I was becoming increasingly dissatisfied with narratives that focused on the journey of a single protagonist. I had a huge appetite for story and no longer felt sated with a singular view but sought out work that attempted a broader coverage of human experience. I was as much interested in the connections between people as in the people themselves. I was fascinated by how tightly woven human experience can be, yet we seem increasingly alienated from one another.

Speaking in Tongues was first performed at the Stables Theatre in Sydney in September 1996. Ray Lawrence was in the audience on opening night. He returned to see the play three of four times over the course of its initial season. He then came to me and suggested the possibility of a film.

Deidre Rubenstein approached me around 1997 to write a piece for her collection of monologues *Confidentially Yours* which she premiered at Playbox in 1998. She gave me an open brief and again I returned to the *Speaking in Tongues* material. Through two monologues I told the story of neighbours Jane and Paula. I reinvented Jane for this version making her an older single woman and brought Paula, the wife of Nik from *Distant Lights*, into this increasingly complex world.

The point of all this history is that by the time I came to write the film I had been carrying these characters and their respective stories for a number of years and had explored them in many guises. Something kept drawing me back to them. The writing of the film then became the denouement of this multifaceted creative process. However, all this preparation didn't make the task any easier. Film is a very different beast and presented me with an entirely new set of demands.

Writing the screenplay became less a process of adaptation than a retelling of the story. I decided early to find a new title. The religious connotation of the play title was always a little obscure. I don't know if 'Lantana' is any clearer but symbolically it gave me the sense of a new beginning. To me the lantana vine visually manifested the inter-weaving and mysterious nature of the story I was trying to tell. It's an impenetrable vine with twisted and entangled branches that conceal a dark interior. It's covered in exquisite and delicate flowers but when you reach in to pick one your hand is cut to shreds by hundreds of tiny thorns. These qualities find their expression in the structure of the story.

I wrote the treatment for Ray and when we felt it was strong enough we took it to Jan Chapman with whom we both had an association through previous work. She responded well to the treatment and came on board as producer. For the next couple of years the three of us steered our way through a labyrinth that really continued all the way to the first large public screening at the opening of the Sydney Film Festival. One of the central themes of the film is trust, yet that quality embodied the three-way relationship between producer, director and writer throughout the development of the script and the making of the film.

I find it difficult to encapsulate all the changes that have been made in the transformation from the play to the film. Writing for me is an organic process where I respond to the impetus of the moment rather than any grand design. Hence it is difficult sometimes to locate the reasons for particular changes. Valerie's disappearance became the instigating event that sits at the core of the story. It is like a stone dropped into a still pond, the ripples circling out and affecting all that they touch. I allowed Leon's journey to become the spine of the film. It could have been any number of other characters but I liked Leon and felt that he had the furthest to fall. In the play the character John has an affair with Sarah who is a client of his wife. As Valerie becomes aware of this she naturally becomes more stricken and is in a particularly vulnerable place on the night she disappears. At some point between draft X and Y it felt that we were tiring of the marital infidelity scenario. It is explored elsewhere in the film, so I sought to complicate it further in the John–Valerie relationship. So Sarah became Patrick and Valerie misreads his motives and wrongly concludes that there is a connection between client and husband. This was a substantial change as an actual threat had been transformed into a perceived threat. It fundamentally changed the nature of the character of Valerie. The John–Valerie relationship is explored further in the film than in the play through a back-story that involves the loss of their daughter. This event has marked their marriage with a grief that they ultimately cannot escape. I was also able to introduce Paula and Nik's marriage into the film, which was only referred to in the play. Paula's faith in Nik in the face of overwhelming evidence against him is an important counterbalance to the crisis of faith being played out in the other relationships. Neil's story, as told in the play, became increasingly difficult to sustain in the film. In the play Leon tells Sonja a story that has been told to him by Neil. In the film I made several attempts to dramatise the passing of this story first from Neil to Leon and then from Leon to Sonja. Despite these attempts it continued to read like a theatrical device. In the play Neil had once had a relationship with Sarah. When Sarah became Patrick Neil's story became even less pertinent. The plot was already complex. Removing Neil from the story liberated it from being unnecessarily so.

In fact Neil was not so much lost as transformed in the film. He became the mysterious man that Leon runs into whilst jogging, which is the premise for the Leon–Neil story. This above all other changes exemplifies the nature of writing. What I considered once to be central to the whole endeavour was distilled into a single shocking moment in the film.

Perhaps the greatest shift though from play to screenplay lies in their differing resolutions. In the play the end is sudden and ambiguous, leaving us uncertain about what actually happened to Valerie. In the film Valerie's fate is revealed. Why one medium demands an open ending and the other demands closure is a question I'm still pondering and is perhaps the subject of a wider discussion to be had elsewhere.

It has been difficult to classify the film according to genre and its complicated multi-plot-lines made it a nightmare to pitch to investors. Yet I'm proud of both these qualities in the face of a film industry that increasingly attempts to reduce any story to a one-sentence logline. Suffice to say *Lantana* is part mystery, part thriller and part journey through the labyrinth of love.

I owe sincere thanks to Ray and Jan who have become good friends as well as collaborators. I also acknowledge the work of the many actors who have played their parts in the many forms this story has taken, none more so than the final ensemble who took on the film with such generosity and insight.

Andrew Bovell
August 2001

MAIN CAST

Leon	ANTHONY LAPAGLIA
John	GEOFFREY RUSH
Valerie	BARBARA HERSHEY
Sonja	KERRY ARMSTRONG
Jane	RACHAEL BLAKE
Nik	VINCE COLOSIMO
Mystery Man	RUSSELL DYKSTRA
Paula	DANIELA FARINACCI
Patrick	PETER PHELPS
Claudia	LEAH PURCELL
Pete	GLENN ROBBINS

Director, Ray Lawrence
Producer, Jan Chapman
Screenplay, Andrew Bovell

Complete film credits appear at the end of the book

How the script relates to the finished film

The published screenplay is the final shooting script delivered by the writer. However, as is generally the case, there were changes made when the film was shot. The significant differences between the screenplay and the finished film are annotated as follows:

1. The scene numbers on the left are the original numbers in the shooting script. Numbers in braces on the right indicate the actual position of the scene in the film.

> SCENE 15 INT. VALERIE'S OFFICE. DAY.   {16} ◄

2. The * symbol indicates that in the film the scene as written formed only part of the scene in the finished film. Thus scripted scenes 102 and 103 each form part of scene 97 in the finished film.

> SCENE 102 EXT. JANE'S STREET. DAY.   {97*} ◄
>
> *Nik is walking along the street pushing the pram. The baby is asleep. He reaches for his pack of cigarettes. They're not there. He pats his pockets, then realises he's forgotten them. He turns and heads back toward the house.*
>
> SCENE 103 EXT. THE VACANT BLOCK. DAY.   {97*} ◄
>
> ► *(Note: in the finished film Jane sees Nik returning for his pack of cigarettes and ducks.)*

3. Major changes in the film that were not in the shooting script are in brackets.

4. Braces around text, whether dialogue or a scene description, indicate it is not included in the finished film. (Note: If a scene from the shooting script was cut from the film it has no final film version scene number.)

> ► {SCENE 169 INT. THE INTERVIEW ROOM – THE POLICE STATION. NIGHT.
>
> NIK: I run. It's dark. So I can't see. I trip and fall. That's how I got these cuts on my face.}

SCENE 1 BLACK   {1}

A thundering chorus of cicadas, the unmistakable sound of summer.

Fade in:

SCENE 2 EXT. LANTANA UNDERGROWTH. DAY.   {2}

{*Tight on the delicate flower of the lantana vine: circling clusters of pink, white and yellow.*}

Pull back through the twisted vine. Shafts of sunlight penetrate the dark undergrowth. It's thick, entangled, covered in thorns and out of control. The air is close. We can hardly breathe. A fly buzzes, loud and insistent. Something dirty and pale is glimpsed through the foliage. Skin.

Slowly the body of a woman is revealed, draped like a cloth through the vine. One foot wears a black leather shoe. The other is bare and pale. There's dried blood between her toes. Her stockings are torn. Her legs are scratched and stained with mud. A black leech sucks on the inside of her calf.

Her face remains concealed. We come to rest on her hands, cupped at her chest. She wears a simple gold wedding band.

Title: 'Lantana'.

The up-beat rhythms of Latin cumbia music drastically change the mood. The music continues over.

SCENE 3 INT. A MOTEL ROOM. DAY.   {3}

Two people making love. Him sliding feverishly into her. She searching for something solid to grip on the bed head. The Latin beat pumps beneath them as the sex builds, then …

SCENE 4 INT. THE MOTEL ROOM. DAY.   {4}

Later. Silence except for the low purr of a clapped-out air conditioner mounted on the wall.

Leon Zat sits on the edge of the unmade bed buttoning his shirt. He's somewhere past forty and fighting to stay fit.

Jane O'May {sits on the other side buttoning her blouse}. She's flushed from the sex and the heat, her hair is tousled and doing its own thing. She feels her earlobe and finds an earring missing. She checks the other lobe revealing a small pearl stud.

She starts to search among the twisted sheets. Leon looks up from tying his shoelace.

LEON: What is it?

JANE: My earring.

> *Leon starts looking too, checking the floor. Jane gets down on her knees and looks under the bed. Leon turns the pillows over.*

LEON: What's it like?

JANE: It's a little pearl. [*Without thinking*] My husband gave them to me.

> *A beat. They look at each other. Awkward. Jane gets up off her knees.*

I'm quite fond of them.

LEON: It'll turn up.

> {*She moves into the adjacent bathroom. She searches through her handbag for a brush. Leon glances at his watch. She catches it in the mirror and says it before he does.*}

JANE: You should go.

> *He reaches for his suit coat.*

LEON: [*apologetically*] Yeah.

> *He moves to the bathroom door. She's brushing her hair in the mirror. She sees him in the mirror, then turns to face him.*

[*Meaning it*] I really enjoyed that.

JANE: So did I.

> *They hold on each other for a beat. And then the cumbia beat starts again and continues over.*

SCENE 5 INT./EXT. LEON'S CAR – CITY STREETS. DUSK. {5}

Leon is driving through traffic. He's running late. {He runs his fingers through the close crop of his hair, then catches sight of himself in the mirror. He looks away.}

He shifts in his seat feeling something uncomfortable down his pants. Keeping one hand on the wheel he reaches in deep and pulls something out. It's the pearl stud. He stares at it.

SCENE 6 EXT. A DANCE STUDIO. DUSK.   {6}

Leon pulls the car into a parking space.

Sonja Zat, Leon's wife, waits outside a city dance studio. She's a handsome woman, forty something. She watches couples and singles, mainly women, going into the studio.

Leon moves along the footpath. He sees Sonja ahead. She hasn't seen him. He stops just to watch her a moment. She's luminous in the last of the day's light. She looks over and sees him. Her face breaks into a warm smile.

SCENE 7 INT. THE DANCE STUDIO. NIGHT.   {7}

The cumbia music plays over a Latin dance class. The instructors, Steve and Lisa, demonstrate the salsa. It's fast, furious and very, very sexy.

The class of beginners watch on daunted but excited. Some move on the spot following the steps, as is the practise. Leon and Sonja stand together. Leon looks uncomfortable. This isn't his scene.

He notices a woman slipping into the class late. It's Jane. There's no acknowledgment between them.

SCENE 8 INT. THE DANCE STUDIO. NIGHT.   {8}

Later. There are more women than men in the class so Jane is partnered with another woman. She watches Sonja and Leon across the room. They look good together like some couples do.

We cut to them as they move tentatively through the routine. Leon is unsure of the steps but Sonja moves with natural poise.

Steve approaches them. He places his hand in the small of Leon's back and moves his groin in.

STEVE: This is about sex, Leon.

> *Jane passes with her partner. Leon glances at her.*

About men and women groin to groin. Get it?

> *Steve steps in, groin to groin with Sonja and moves her expertly across the floor. There's a spark between them. A rush moves through the room. Sonja feels the excitement of being confidently led. She gives into it willingly. The other dancers clear the floor to watch.*

> *Leon looks on somewhere between pissed off and embarrassed. It's like watching another man make love to your wife and realising that she enjoys it more with him than you.*

SCENE 9 EXT. A STREET. MORNING.   {9}

Leon pounds the empty footpath, jogging. His face runs with sweat. He's doing all he can to keep age at bay. (Note: in the finished film Leon feels a twinge of chest pain.)

SCENE 10 INT. THE LAUNDRY – LEON AND SONJA'S HOUSE. MORNING.   {10}

Sonja's ironing a blouse for work. She's dressed in a skirt and bra.

SAM: [*out of view*] Mum …
SONJA: In here.

> *Sam, sixteen, appears in pyjama bottoms.*

SAM: I haven't got any clothes.
SONJA: Have you looked on your bedroom floor?
SAM: I mean clean ones.
SONJA: If you pick them up, I'll wash them.

> *Leon comes to the back door, sweaty and breathing hard from the run. He*

counts his pulse with his finger on his wrist.

SAM: You shouldn't jog … It's dangerous.

LEON: I want to get fit.

SAM: What for?

LEON: [*slipping off his runners*] I don't want to die.

SONJA: [*ironing*] You are going to die.

LEON: Yeah, but I don't want to die yet.

SONJA: Then stop jogging.

SCENE 11 INT. THE KITCHEN – LEON AND SONJA'S HOUSE. MORNING.   {11}

Sonja is cleaning up. Sam and Dylan, fourteen, are dressed for school and finishing breakfast. Leon comes in dressed for work.

DYLAN: [*rising*] Got to go.

> *Dylan grabs his bag and kisses Sonja and then Leon goodbye. Sam kisses Sonja and is about to follow Dylan out the door.*

LEON: What about me?

SAM: Dad … I'm sixteen.

LEON: So? What're you telling me? That you're a man now?

SAM: No.

> *Leon gestures, 'Well?' Sam relents without animosity, kisses Leon goodbye and leaves. Leon watches him go.*

LEON: Is there some point when a son stops kissing his father?

SONJA: Apparently.

> {*She kisses him goodbye and leaves. Leon stands in the stillness of the room, reflective. His boys are getting older, but so is he. He puts the breakfast cereal away.*}

SCENE 12 INT. A RUN-DOWN HOUSE. DAY.   {12}

{*A man's face is slammed into the wall. The hand doing the shoving belongs to Leon. He pulls the man's arm behind his back and cuffs him.*

6

LEON: What'd you say?}

> *(Note: in the finished film Leon chases a man through the house and kicks him on the ground.) Claudia, thirties, Leon's partner, looks over. We're in the middle of a drug bust. The room is swarming with cops. Two other men are being apprehended. A table is littered with drug paraphernalia.*

{You say something to me?

> *The man's face contorts with pain as Leon bends his arm back. Claudia moves in and takes over. She marches him out the door.*}

SCENE 13 EXT. THE RUN-DOWN HOUSE. DAY. {13}

{*Claudia puts the man in the back of a police car and closes the door. She looks back as Leon emerges from the house. She joins him as they walk to their car.*} *(Note: in the finished film we see police officers escort the men to the car. Leon and Claudia are in their car.)*

CLAUDIA: You went in a bit hard, {didn't you?}

LEON: The guy's a pusher.

CLAUDIA: Yeah, but he wasn't going anywhere.

> *Leon opens the car door.*

LEON: What did you want me to do, {Claudia? Be polite to him?

> *He gets into the car and slams the door. Claudia raises her eyes before she gets into the car.*}

SCENE 14 INT./EXT. AN UNMARKED POLICE CAR – CITY STREETS. DAY. {15}

(Note: in the finished film Scene 14 establishes the police station exterior and the following scene takes place inside the station.) {*Leon is at the wheel. Claudia is in the passenger seat. They move through city traffic in an uneasy silence. Leon tries to recover.*}

LEON: You seeing anyone yet?

CLAUDIA: Not with the hours I keep.

LEON: What about someone on the force?

CLAUDIA: Male cops are lousy in bed.

Leon smirks.

There is someone.

Leon looks across ... interested. Claudia is a little tentative.

He eats in the same restaurant as I do.

LEON: Have you spoken to him?

CLAUDIA: We've exchanged glances.

Leon looks dubious.

It's a start.

Leon smiles. There's the easy warmth of friendship between them.

How's Sonja?

LEON: Good.

CLAUDIA: I haven't seen her for a while.

A beat, then Leon shrugs it off.

LEON: She's busy; you know, work, the boys.

SCENE 15 INT. VALERIE'S OFFICE. DAY.   {16}

Tight on Sonja's face. She's sitting in a therapist's office.

VALERIE: [*out of view*] Have you told him you're not happy?

SONJA: I thought that maybe he wouldn't need to be told.

Valerie Somers, forties, smiles with a therapist's calm assurance.

VALERIE: That depends on how good an actor you are.

SONJA: I guess I'm pretty good.

Valerie waits a moment, allowing Sonja to gather her thoughts. A small tape recorder sits on the table between them.

VALERIE: How do you want your marriage to be, {Sonja}?

SONJA: Passionate. Challenging. Honest.

VALERIE: Isn't it honest?

SONJA: Not emotionally, no. I feel like we're just going through the motions ... I want more than that.

{SCENE 16 EXT. A CITY LANEWAY. EVENING.

A man moves the butt of a broken bottle aside with the toe of his black, polished shoe. He is John Knox, forties, well groomed. He wears a suit; his hair is starting to grey.

His eyes settle on a place further down the laneway – a discarded mattress lies against a rusted tin fence, tufts of weed push through the concrete, the ground is strewn with broken glass and crushed cigarette packets – one of life's forgotten and forlorn places.

The sound of a mobile phone ringing in John's car jars the silence. He doesn't register it. His eyes remain fixed on the laneway ahead.}

SCENE 17 EXT. VALERIE'S OFFICE. EVENING.   {17}

{*Valerie stands on the footpath outside her office. She lowers the mobile phone from her ear and turns it off. Something across the street catches her eye.*}

A girl, in school uniform and ponytail, stands at a bus stop.

Valerie smiles {as she watches her pull a ribbon from her hair, causing it to fall across her shoulders}. The girl looks across and notices Valerie watching her.

Valerie quickly looks away. A taxi pulls up. She gets into the back seat {and the taxi pulls into traffic.}

MAN: [*voice over*] Ladies and gentlemen, please welcome Dr Valerie Somers.

SCENE 18 INT. THE FUNCTION ROOM – A HOTEL.
NIGHT.   {18}

Valerie moves through the room to the applause of people standing with drinks in their hands. She's smiling, confident and assured, but her eyes search the room, looking for someone.

{*A man, Patrick Phelan, watches her from the crowd as she moves through the room. She reaches the podium and shakes the hand of the man who introduced her.*}

She faces the audience, waiting for their applause to settle.

VALERIE: Thank you …

SCENE 19 INT. THE FOYER – THE HOTEL. NIGHT.   {19}

John comes through the hotel doors in a hurry. He's running late. He moves through the hotel foyer. Outside the function room is a blown-up poster on a display stand. It is the cover of a book depicting a young girl under the title Eleanor, *by Dr Valerie Somers. John passes it on his way in.*

SCENE 20 INT. THE FUNCTION ROOM – THE HOTEL. NIGHT.   {20}

John enters to see Valerie already speaking at the podium.

VALERIE: We don't know what to feel any more. We don't know what's right or wrong any more. The cry of the modern age. {Or not so much a cry, but a scream.}

    She plays her audience well. They give her rapt attention.

We ask, 'What should we believe in?' Our politicians? Hardly. Our priests? You'd be amazed at how many of my clients come to see me because they once believed in a priest.

    A ripple of uneasy laughter moves through the room.

Our parents? Home is a sanctuary for a privileged few. For most it's a battleground. Love?

    Valerie sees John at the back of the room. Their eyes meet.

Is that what makes us feel safe in this world?

    Patrick watches her.

Loving someone requires the relinquishment of power. Doesn't it? It's about surrender. Mutual surrender. But on what basis can this take place?

    John watches her.

Trust. It's as vital to the conduct of human relationships as breath is to life … and just as elusive.

    Valerie pauses. John watches the emotion build in her eyes.

Two years ago my twelve-year-old daughter was murdered.

This is difficult for him. He feels the anticipation build in the room. This is what they've come to hear.

Her name was 'Eleanor'.

(Note: in the finished film, Eleanor is eleven.)

SCENE 21 INT./EXT. JOHN'S CAR – A COASTAL FREEWAY. NIGHT.   {21}

John is at the wheel. Valerie watches the freeway lights sweep along limestone cliffs. They travel in silence.

JOHN: It seemed to go well.
VALERIE: I thought you weren't going to make it.
{JOHN: I was running late.
VALERIE: I tried calling you.}

John keeps his eyes on the road. (Note: in the finished film John squeezes Valerie's hand and says 'I said I would be'.) {The freeway cuts through the black like a knife. She looks across at him. She watches the lights play across his face then lets it go. She looks back out the window. Up ahead she sees an exit from the freeway loom before them.

SCENE 22 EXT. THE COASTAL FREEWAY. NIGHT.

John's car rushes past the freeway exit. We stay on it. It's menacing, like the entrance to a dark tunnel.}

SCENE 23 INT. ELEANOR'S ROOM – VALERIE AND JOHN'S HOUSE. NIGHT.   {22}

Valerie {strikes a match in the darkened room and} lights a candle {floating in a bowl of water}. It's placed on the table beneath the window. The flame illuminates the room and reveals a number of photos on the table, capturing Eleanor at various ages.

{Valerie sits on the bed and watches the shadows move across the walls.} It's a young girl's room, posters on the walls, hats and scarves draped on the hooks. Books, dolls,

ornaments and trinkets neatly placed on shelves, a time capsule holding her daughter's life still.

John comes to the door. He has a glass of whisky in his hand.

JOHN: Do you want a drink?

VALERIE: I've got an early client.

JOHN: Why don't we take separate cars in the morning?

> *Valerie hesitates. The suggestion is unexpected.*

I've got a late meeting. That way you won't have to wait in town for me.

VALERIE: It's fine. I've got work I can do. You can pick me up after your meeting.

> *A beat on John – thwarted. There's nothing he can do but agree.*

JOHN: [*smiling*] Okay.

> *He turns and leaves the room. Valerie stares at the empty space in the doorway, shadows from the candle moving across her face.*

SCENE 24 INT. VALERIE'S OFFICE. DAY. {23}

Patrick sits opposite Valerie. A tape recorder sits on the table, recording the session.

PATRICK: I met someone. We went home and had sex. As you do.

> *Valerie smiles – a hint of irony.*

Well, some of us do. And then he asked to see me again. I wasn't expecting that.

VALERIE: And?

PATRICK: Well, against my better judgment, I said 'Yes'.

> *Valerie smiles, pleased for him.*

Anyway, we've been seeing each other for a while.

VALERIE: And you like him?

PATRICK: Yeah, I do. Very much.

VALERIE: [*sensing a catch*] So?

PATRICK: He comes encumbered … with a wife.

> *She feels a pang of discomfort. It's the word 'encumbered'. Professionally, she puts it aside.*

VALERIE: Is he gay?

PATRICK: Well, when he's with me he seems to be.

VALERIE: Does she know about you?

PATRICK: I assume so. She would sense it … wouldn't she?

VALERIE: It depends on how good he is at deceiving her.

PATRICK: Or how good she is at deceiving herself.

> *She falters a moment; not that Patrick sees it. She has mastered the therapist's facade of control.*

{If this was just some bored husband flirting with his dark side it wouldn't matter. I would know where I stand. But I've done something stupid, Valerie. I've fallen in love with the man. The question is, can I have him? Do I have the right?}

> *(Note: in the finished film an unscripted Scene 24 establishes Jane's house, craning up out of a lantana thicket.)*

SCENE 25 INT./EXT. JANE'S HOUSE. EVENING.   {25}

A slow salsa fills the house. We find Jane dancing barefoot on the carpet, the soles of her feet pressing deep into the pile. She's practising the steps from the dance class. She stops, feeling a little self-conscious. She moves to the window and sips from her glass of white wine. Outside she can see her neighbour Nik D'Amato working under the bonnet of his car in his driveway. He's in his late twenties. He wears old jeans and no shirt. Jane lingers on him a moment.

SCENE 26 EXT. THE FRONT YARD – NIK AND PAULA'S HOUSE. EVENING.   {26}

{*Nik concentrates on the carburettor; his hands are stained with grease.*} *The music can be heard coming from Jane's house.* {*The sky is pink, a forewarning of tomorrow's heat.*}

Paula, his wife, is sitting on the front steps sipping a beer. She wears her nurse's uniform hitched up to catch the breeze. She's listening to Hannah, their six-year-old daughter, struggling through her school reader. She's trying to be patient but keeps jumping in to prompt her.

PAULA: It's 'apple'. Look at the picture.
HANNAH: Let me do it, Mum.

> *(Note: in the finished film Hannah is learning "U" for "umbrella" and 'V'.) Their other kids, George, four, and Harry, about eighteen months, are playing on the lawn. Nik looks up to see Jane coming out onto her porch. She brings her glass of wine.*

NIK: You having a party in there, Jane?
JANE: Yeah … want to join me?

> *Jane crosses into their yard and moves up the drive. Paula glances up from listening to Hannah read.*

PAULA: [*to Hannah*] {That's enough, babe.} We'll do the rest in the morning.

> *Jane sits down on the steps beside Paula. She smiles as Hannah scoots off inside with the can. Paula fixes on Jane, a serious look.*

Well?

> *Jane glances over to Nik, checking he's out of earshot. She nods with an embarrassed grin.*

Where?
JANE: A motel.

> *Paula squeals with vicarious delight. Nik glances up from under the bonnet.*

PAULA: Did you get his number?
JANE: Is that what you do?
PAULA: Well, I'm no expert, but if you liked him …
JANE: [*a little defensively*] He's married.

> *Paula winces a little.*

PAULA: So, what … ? He's not happy?
JANE: I don't know. He can't be, can he?
PAULA: You going to see him again?
JANE: Do you think I should?
PAULA: Do you want me to be honest?
JANE: No.
{PAULA: Tell him to sort out his marriage. If he and his wife are going to split, then, fine, otherwise you're just a part of his mid-life crisis.}

> *Jane twists the gold band on her finger. She knows Paula's right.*

When are you going to take that thing off?
JANE: It's too tight. I've got to get it cut off.

> {*Harry has wandered over. Jane lifts him onto her knee. Cicadas fill the air with their constant song, seeming to get louder.*}

PAULA: Nik caught up with Pete the other day.

> *Jane resists the temptation to ask.*

He wants to come back.

> *She shakes her head, clear about that much, at least.*

JANE: I don't love him, Paula.

SCENE 27 EXT. THE POLICE STATION. NIGHT.   {27^A}

Leon and Claudia come out of the building and start walking down the street. They are mid-conversation.

LEON: Just go over to his table and ask him to join you. You've got nothing to lose.
CLAUDIA: Just a little dignity.
LEON: I don't think dignity's an issue. The man eats alone in a restaurant.
CLAUDIA: So do I.
LEON: Exactly.

SCENE 28 INT./EXT. JANE'S CAR – A STREET. NIGHT. {27*}

Jane is sitting in her car. She's watching Leon and Claudia walk down the street. She gets out and walks toward them as though she just happens to be there.

Leon sees her moving toward them. He's immediately conscious of Claudia. Jane stops and feigns surprise.

JANE: Hi.

> *Claudia looks from Jane to Leon, seeking an introduction.*

LEON: Hi … Ah, Claudia … Jane.
JANE: Hi.

> *Claudia nods politely; she smells a rat.*

LEON: Jane's … doing the same dancing classes as us.

Claudia nods. Jane's not moving on. Claudia gets the gist.

CLAUDIA: I'll get going. *[Moving off]* Say 'Hi' to Sonja.

Leon shoots a glance at the back of Claudia's head.

LEON: Yeah.

JANE: Sorry … Was that awkward?

LEON: No. It's fine … How are you?

JANE: Good.

She's not. There's an awkward silence.

{I was just doing some shopping.

Leon nods.} Jane regrets having done this.

I better get going.

She moves off. Leon fights the temptation to say something. Jane keeps walking, hoping he'll call her back. Leon is about to walk on when he remembers something. He reaches into his coat pocket.

LEON: Jane …

She turns around to see Leon holding the pearl earring in the palm of his hand. She smiles. Their eyes meet.

SCENE 29 INT. A VIETNAMESE RESTAURANT. NIGHT. {28}

Claudia sits at a table alone. Most of the tables are filled with couples or families. She looks up at the sound of the door. {A young couple enter and look for a table.} Claudia looks away. She finishes her soup, takes ten dollars from her wallet and leaves it on the table.

SCENE 30 EXT. THE VIETNAMESE RESTAURANT. NIGHT.
{29}

Claudia steps out into the street and starts to walk away. She hears the door of the restaurant open behind her. She glances back to see the man stepping into the restaurant. She watches him through the restaurant window. We don't see his face. He takes a table and sits alone. Claudia smiles at the missed opportunity – story of her life – and walks on.

SCENE 31 EXT. JANE'S HOUSE. NIGHT.   {30}

Leon's car is parked outside the house. Nik is pushing the pram, returning from walking the baby to sleep. As he passes the house he notes Leon's car with interest.

SCENE 32 INT. THE KITCHEN – NIK AND PAULA'S HOUSE. NIGHT.   {31}

{Paula is stuffing clothes into a washing machine.} Like most working mothers she looks wrung out. The kitchen's a mess. Dishes not done. Dirty clothes and toys on the floor. Nik comes in.

NIK: There's an unmarked police car next door.

PAULA: So?

NIK: Is she seeing a cop, now?

PAULA: Don't be nosey. [*Glancing at the pram*] Asleep?

> *He nods.*

NIK: So are she and Pete getting back together or what?

PAULA: I don't know.

> *Paula starts clearing away the dinner things.*

NIK: Well, what if they do? What do we say then?

PAULA: Nothing.

NIK: Yeah, but he's a mate of mine.

PAULA: Then do him a favour and stay out of it.

SCENE 33 INT. THE MAIN BEDROOM – JANE'S HOUSE. NIGHT.   {32}

Jane and Leon are making love on the bed. Jane is on her knees, Leon's thrusts causing Jane to bang her head on the headboard.

LEON: Fuck … Sorry.

Leah Purcell as Claudia in *Lantana*. (Photo: Elise Lockwood.)

JANE: Don't stop … Don't …

> *Leon resumes thrusting. He grabs a pillow and stuffs it between Jane's head and the headboard.*

Ta …

> *Leon keeps thrusting, building the intensity for them both. Suddenly he stops thrusting and grabs his chest. Jane looks back over her shoulder. Leon pulls away. He's in pain.*

Leon … ?

> *Leon doubles over to ease the pain.*

What is it?

LEON: Nothing … I just get this pain in my chest.

> *But his face is full of panic.*

JANE: Should I call a doctor?

> *He sits up and breathes through the pain. He shakes his head.*

You should have told me you had a weak heart.

LEON: I haven't …

JANE: Of all the men to have an affair with …

LEON: For Christ sake, I'm telling you I haven't got a weak heart. And it's not an affair. It's a one-night stand. Except that it's happened twice.

> *Jane stares at him.*

Shit … I didn't mean that.

> *She moves to him, kisses the back of his neck. She wraps her arms around his shoulders and holds him tight. She doesn't want to let him go. Leon feels uncomfortable with the embrace. Fucking's one thing, emotional need is another.*

SCENE 34 EXT. NIK AND PAULA'S HOUSE. NIGHT.   {33}

Nik is working under the bonnet of his car as Leon comes out of Jane's house. Nik watches him get into his car and drive away.

SCENE 35 INT./EXT. JOHN'S CAR – THE COASTAL FREEWAY. NIGHT.   {34}

The car is travelling at speed along the freeway. John and Valerie travel in silence. The road cuts through the dark like a knife. Finally Valerie speaks.

VALERIE: Does it worry you that we don't have sex very often?

The question is unexpected. John takes it in his stride.

JOHN: No … I mean, I don't think about it that much.

VALERIE: Why not?

JOHN: I love you. Whether we make love three times a week or once a month doesn't really change that.

Valerie looks across at him.

VALERIE: Doesn't it?

She holds on him a moment.

JOHN: Is this a test?

VALERIE: No. I just want to know what you're thinking.

{JOHN: I'm not one of your clients, Valerie.}

Valerie looks back out the window. (Note: in the finished film John asks why women want to know that.) {The headlights of an oncoming car appear in the darkness.

SCENE 36 EXT. THE COASTAL FREEWAY. NIGHT.

The two cars pass on the freeway.

SCENE 37 INT./EXT. LEON'S CAR – THE COASTAL FREEWAY. NIGHT.

We are now inside the other car – with Leon, driving back from Jane's house. His eyes are fixed on the road ahead.}

SCENE 38 INT. LEON AND SONJA'S HOUSE. NIGHT. {35}

The front door opens and Leon enters. He listens for a sign that anyone is awake. The house is quiet. There's a light on in the kitchen. He moves down the hall.

Sonja looks up from the table. There are open books and paper on the table. She's studying. She wears Leon's pyjamas.

LEON: You're up late.
SONJA: [*looking down*] Trying to finish this.

> *Leon looks over her shoulder at the work. He kisses her on the forehead.*

LEON: Do you want {a cup of tea?}
SONJA: Just had one.

> {*He switches on the kettle and waits for the sound of the water starting to heat. The silence between them is tense.*

LEON: Boys asleep?

> *She nods. Silence until the kettle starts to boil. Leon doesn't react. Sonja looks up at the sound, prompting Leon to switch it off. He dumps a teabag in a cup and pours on the water.*} *(Note: in the finished film Leon has a drink.)*

SONJA: What's wrong?
LEON: Nothing.

> *There are beads of sweat on his forehead.*

It was a shit of a day. I stopped off and had a drink with Claudia.
SONJA: Yeah, I phoned her.

> *Leon tenses.*

I wasn't sure if you were working late.

> *Sonja looks at him, saying nothing. He nearly cracks. She looks back to her work. Leon sips his tea. They fall back into silence.*

SCENE 39 EXT. THE FOOTPATH. EARLY MORNING. {36}

Leon is jogging tight against a brick wall. Sweat pours from his face, veins bulge from his neck. He increases his pace, building to a sprint. He reaches a corner, then SMACK. The crunch of bone. He runs straight into a man coming around the corner.

The collision is brutal. The man falls to the ground. Leon regains his balance and lets forth with a torrent of abuse.

LEON: You fucking idiot. What the fuck do you think you're doing?

> *He holds his hand to his head and sees that he's bleeding.*

{Jesus fucking Christ.}

> *The man cowers under Leon's booming voice. He instinctively raises his hand to shield himself as though he expects to be struck. This shocks Leon to silence. He backs off, regains control. He's shocked by his overreaction.*

Shit … Look, I'm sorry …

> *{He reaches to help but the man pushes his hand away and gets to his feet.} Blood is running from his nose and lip. (Note: in the finished film Leon picks up the man's shopping and he snatches it.)*

Are you alright?

> *The man doesn't reply, {he just wants to get away. Leon watches him go. He is about to move on when he sees the man stop and steady himself against the wall.} And then it happens, violent and shocking. The man gasps, overtaken by emotion, and sobs, his hands covering his bloodied face.*

> *Leon is unsure what to do. He looks around as though he needs someone else to tell him. There's nobody. {He approaches tentatively,} finding the rawness of the man's emotion difficult to confront. The man can't look at him; the presence of a stranger only makes it worse.*

> *{Leon reaches out to reassure him. The man's legs buckle. Leon grabs him under the arms as he collapses into him.} He buries his face into Leon's shoulder. Leon holds him, bewildered as he weeps.*

> *{Finally the man pulls away. He meets Leon's eye for a brief moment, then looks away, ashamed. He quickly starts to walk away. He disappears around the corner. Leon is left stunned; the man's blood is on his T-shirt and the side of his face.}*

SCENE 40 INT. THE LAUNDRY AND HALL – LEON AND SONJA'S HOUSE. MORNING.   {37, 38*}

(Note: in the finished film the scene takes place in the kitchen.) Leon comes to the back door. {He slips his runners off.} Blood has mixed with sweat and streaks his face and T-shirt with grime. He moves through the laundry into a hallway and passes Sonja walking down the hall. She sees his face.

SONJA: What happened?

> *Leon keeps moving.*

LEON: I fell.

SCENE 41 INT. THE BATHROOM – LEON AND SONJA'S HOUSE. MORNING.   {38*}

Leon comes into the bathroom. Sonja follows him.

SONJA: Are you okay?
LEON: Yeah.

> *He strips off his T-shirt.*

SONJA: [*approaching*] Let me look at it.
LEON: [*backing off*] It's nothing.
SONJA: Leon …
LEON: I said I'm alright.

> *Sonja is taken aback by the abruptness of his response. She leaves the bathroom. Leon catches himself in the mirror. He sees the dried blood on the side of his face. He is vulnerable and completely unnerved.*

SCENE 42 INT. VALERIE'S OFFICE. DAY.   {39}

Valerie is with Patrick. The session has been going for some time.

PATRICK: I think about her a lot.
VALERIE: Are you feeling guilty?

PATRICK: Do you think I should be?

VALERIE: It doesn't matter what I think, Patrick.

Patrick meets her eye – as if to say, that's not true and she knows it. He lets it go.

PATRICK: He feels manipulated by her.

VALERIE: How?

PATRICK: She's very needy.

VALERIE: Are you trying to justify his deceit?

PATRICK: I'm trying to understand it, that's all. It's complex.

VALERIE: But it's still an act of deceit, isn't it? No marriage can be based on that.

PATRICK: Most marriages are based on that, Valerie.

VALERIE: Do you think you would know?

PATRICK: What, because I'm gay I can't have an opinion on the state of contemporary marriage?

VALERIE: I didn't mean to suggest that.

PATRICK: She's not a victim in this. She chose to marry him.

VALERIE: Not knowing he was gay.

PATRICK: There's knowing and there's knowing.

VALERIE: What do you mean?

PATRICK: I think some women go along with the lie. It's easier than dealing with the truth.

Valerie feels uncomfortable, compelled to defend the woman.

VALERIE: Maybe she loves him.

PATRICK: But so do I.

VALERIE: Then he has to make a choice.

PATRICK: Unless one of us withdraws from the contest.

VALERIE: Is love a contest for you, Patrick?

Patrick doesn't reply. We glimpse something more raw inside.

Patrick?

He meets her eye. She feels some kind of challenge.

PATRICK: Yes … Sometimes.

SCENE 43 INT. THE POLICE STATION. DAY.   {40}

Black coffee squirts into a polystyrene cup. {Leon stands at the coffee machine waiting for his cup to fill. There's a ripening bruise on his head.} (Note: in the finished film Claudia pours coffee and gives it to Leon as he enters.)

Above the machine posters of missing people adorn the walls – haunting portraits of young women, children, adult men.

CLAUDIA: {[*out of view*]} What happened to your head?

{*Leon moves aside to let Claudia get to the machine.*}

LEON: I bumped it on the clothesline.

{*Claudia smiles. Leon puts two sugars into his coffee.*}

Thanks … [*Awkwardly*] For last night.

CLAUDIA: I'll lie for you to anyone … Except Sonja. I've done it once. I won't do it again.

Leon nods, it's understood. {*He goes to move back to his desk.*}

Why are you trying so hard to fuck·up your life at the moment?

Leon looks back at her, conscious of other people being around.

You don't know how lucky you are to have the marriage you've got and you're pissing all over it.

Claudia goes, leaving Leon pissed off, but he knows she's right.

{SCENE 44 INT./EXT. LEON'S CAR – CITY STREETS. DUSK.

Leon is driving through heavy traffic. He's anxious. He looks at his watch. He's running late. He stares at the road ahead. He leans on his horn.

LEON: Move, fuck you.}

SCENE 45 EXT. THE DANCE STUDIO. DUSK.   {41}

Leon moves along the footpath. He sees the dance studio up ahead. {He looks for Sonja; she's not waiting for him in her usual spot. Something feels wrong.}

SCENE 46   INT. THE DANCE STUDIO. DUSK.   {42*}

Leon {dashes up the steps. He can hear the music coming from the studio. He} enters and scans the room. His heart skips a beat when he sees that Sonja is dancing with Jane. He watches them a moment, rigid; they're talking as they dance.

Steve partners him up with another woman. There's nothing he can do but watch helplessly as his wife and mistress do the mambo.

{We cut to their feet as they move through the routine – both women are wearing black shoes. We tilt up their bodies.

JANE: You're good at this.
SONJA: Thanks.
JANE: I'm Jane, by the way.
SONJA: Sonja.

> *Leon keeps watching. From his point of view we see Jane look across. Cut back to Jane and Sonja.}*

JANE: It's great that your husband comes with you.

> *Sonja looks over at Leon dancing. She notices the wedding ring on Jane's finger.*

SONJA: What about yours?
JANE: I'm separated.

> *Sonja doesn't say anything.*

Does it show?
SONJA: You have a certain look.
JANE: What, desperate?
SONJA: No. Full of potential.

> *Leon looks across. He sees them laughing. It's excruciating. The song ends. Leon excuses himself from his partner. He moves across the room. He can see them still talking as he approaches.*

LEON: Sorry, I got held up.

> *He kisses Sonja and gives Jane a warning look at the same time. He takes Sonja's arm and manoeuvres her away. Sonja glances back, apologetically. Jane watches them go. (Note: in the finished film Sonja introduces Leon and Jane.) {The music starts.*

STEVE: Salsa, everybody. Let's see those feet moving.

> *Leon and Sonja move into the routine. Leon's all over the place. His mind isn't exactly on his feet. He stops.*

LEON: I can't do this.

> *Sonja senses his discomfort is about more than simply being unable to dance.*

SONJA: Follow me ...

> *Sonja takes the lead. Leon resists.*

Trust me.

> *Leon meets her eye, tentatively starting to get the steps with Sonja's lead. Jane moves around the edges of the room, watching them.*

SCENE 47 INT. THE DANCE STUDIO. NIGHT.   {42*}

Later.} The class is over. Steve is making an announcement.

STEVE: Listen up. There's a cumbia band playing at the Latin tonight. {The only way you're going to get good at this is to practise. I want to see you all there.}

> *(Note: in the finished film Steve announces a Salsa band.) Leon is helping Sonja on with her coat as Steve approaches.*

You guys going to come?

> *Sonja looks at Leon. She'd like to.*

LEON: I thought we might go out and have a meal.
STEVE: Come on, Leon, you can go out and eat any time.

> *Leon would like to punch his head in as Steve moves on.*

SONJA: I'd like to go.
LEON: I'm kind of tired.

> *Sonja pauses a moment. Once she would have deferred to him.*

SONJA: Alright, then ... I'll see you at home.

> *He didn't expect that. She kisses him and leaves to join the others. He looks over and sees Jane delaying her departure, obviously waiting for him.*

LEON: [*approaching*] What the hell was that about?

JANE: She needed a partner.
LEON: And you just happened to volunteer.
JANE: She chose me.

> *Leon doesn't like it.*

I wouldn't say anything, Leon.

> *Leon lets it go. They're silent, not wanting to go but not knowing how to stay.*

SCENE 48 EXT. JANE'S HOUSE. NIGHT.   {43}

{Pete, Jane's husband, is parked in his car, looking at the house. There are no lights on inside.} The sound of cicadas fills the night. He gets out of the car and approaches the house. As he walks through the garden the cicadas fall silent.

SCENE 49 INT. JANE'S HOUSE. NIGHT.   {44}

Pete opens the front door with his key. He turns on a light and looks at the familiar surrounds. He moves into the bedroom, switches on the light and looks at the unmade bed. He hesitates, then can't help himself. He pulls back the sheets, looking for a sign that his wife's love has moved somewhere else. (Note: in the finished film he picks up the pearl earrings from the dressing table.)

SCENE 50 EXT. THE FRONT YARD – NIK AND PAULA'S
HOUSE. NIGHT.   {45}

Nik is working on a car engine set up on blocks as Pete comes down the side of the house. Nik looks up.

NIK: Pete.

> *He wipes his hand on a rag and takes Pete's hand.*

PETE: G'day, Nik. Just called over to see Jane. Looks like she's out.

> *Nik looks in the direction of Jane's house and nods.*

You seen her tonight?

NIK: No, sorry.

PETE: You don't know where she'd be, then?

NIK: No.

> *(Note: in the finished film Pete asks Nik how Jane is, and Nik replies that she is okay.)*

PETE: It's just that it's late. I thought she'd be home.

NIK: I haven't seen her, mate.

> *There's an awkward beat.*

PETE: You'd tell me wouldn't you, Nik, if you thought there was something I should know?

> *Nik nods, hating himself for lying.*

It's just, if she was seeing someone, I'd want to know.

NIK: Sure.

> *Pete starts to go. He hesitates but doesn't look back.*

PETE: I fucking hate this.

> *Nik watches him go, feeling bad for the betrayal.*

SCENE 51 INT. A RESTAURANT. NIGHT.   {47}

Valerie and John are sitting at a table eating a meal. Valerie is playing with her food. (Note: in the finished film the scene begins with John speaking about his work.)

JOHN: You seem preoccupied.

VALERIE: I'm having trouble with a client. I'm not handling him very well.

> *John looks up from his meal.*

JOHN: Refer him on.

> *She knows that's what she should do, but it's not what she needs to hear at the moment. John returns to his meal.*

VALERIE: I find him a little threatening.

JOHN: Why?

VALERIE: I don't like ... what he's doing.

JOHN: You're judging him.

> *She doesn't deny it.*

You have to refer him on, Valerie.

She looks away, distracted by the noise and the heat in the restaurant.

VALERIE: I'm sorry ... Can we go?

Valerie rises abruptly from the table and moves away. John watches her move toward the door before reaching for his wallet.

SCENE 52   EXT. A STREET. NIGHT.   {48}

John comes out of the restaurant. He looks for Valerie and sees her across the street, standing at a shop window. He crosses the street and approaches her.

Close on Valerie's face staring at the shop window. John sees what she's looking at. The image of their daughter is blown up in a window display advertising Valerie's book.

VALERIE: What's happened to us?

John is silent.

We don't talk any more.

JOHN: We lost our daughter.

VALERIE: I thought that would have bought us closer.

She reaches down and takes his hand. She brings it to her lips.

Do you think about her much?

JOHN: Every day.

She looks at him, needing to know.

VALERIE: Do you?

John looks at her, a little angry.

JOHN: Of course I do. I just didn't need to write a book about it.

Valerie is stung.

VALERIE: Do you think I did the wrong thing?

He doesn't answer.

I just wanted the world to know ...

{JOHN: [*forgiving her*] I know.}

He takes her in an embrace.

{VALERIE: John ... Make love to me tonight.}

SCENE 53 INT. A BAR. NIGHT.   {46}

Leon and Jane are sitting at a table in a bar. Leon nurses a whisky, Jane a white wine.

LEON: Why'd you and your husband split up? Do you mind me asking?

    She shakes her head.

JANE: I grew up and realised I was living with a man who I didn't love.

LEON: Was it that simple?

JANE: No.

    Jane laughs a little to cover the obvious pain of it.

LEON: But you knew that much, at least?

    She nods.

JANE: Perhaps my expectations were too high.

    She unconsciously twists the wedding band on her finger.

{Maybe once you reach a certain age love shouldn't be the crucial thing any more.

    She shrugs.

But it still is to me. I can't help it.}

LEON: You're a brave woman. Most people settle for less.

    She thinks maybe he's talking about himself. She's encouraged.

JANE: I'm starting to like you Leon … Maybe too much.

    She caresses the back of his hand on the table.

I'm starting to wonder where this might go.

    Her hand slips down to Leon's leg and moves up his thigh. Leon watches it, fighting his own arousal. Something settles in him.

LEON: I'm still in love with my wife, Jane.

    Jane withdraws her hand.

I'm sorry.

    She grabs hold of her glass for something to hold onto. She's reeling from it.

JANE: Then …why have you been seeing me?

LEON: I don't know. It's not something I planned.

    They sit in silence. Jane feels so exposed.

Look … it doesn't have to end {badly}.

> *She holds up her hand to stop him talking. Leon doesn't move, wanting to resolve it somehow.*

JANE: Just go.

> *He gets up and hesitates, wanting it to be alright.*

Go.

> *He leaves. Jane sips from her glass, feeling forty, vulnerable and very much alone.*

SCENE 54 INT. THE BEDROOM – VALERIE AND JOHN'S HOUSE. NIGHT.   {49}

John and Valerie are making love. Valerie is acutely aware of John but senses that he is somewhere else. His head is averted. His eyes are closed. He's caught in the throes of his own passion.

As John moves to climax she takes his face in his hands and turns it toward her.

VALERIE: Look at me, John … Look at me.

> *He opens his eyes and looks deep into hers. The moment is painful for them both; a glimpse into the damaged soul of the other. John's eyes smart with tears, he blinks them back. Valerie cries as he comes inside her.*
>
> *He pulls away. They lie side by side, shaken and estranged.*
>
> *Dissolve to black.*

SCENE 55 EXT. A VACANT BLOCK. MORNING.   {50}

We're moving through the dark and entangled undergrowth of lantana. Cicadas fill the air. Sparkling grabs of morning sun penetrate through twisted bows. Suddenly two children burst into view, laughing. It's Paula's and Nik's kids, Hannah and George. (Note: in the finished film Nik, out of shot, calls to the children 'Come on, kids. We're late for school'.)

SCENE 56 EXT. THE FRONT YARDS – JANE'S HOUSE AND PAULA AND NIK'S HOUSE. MORNING.   {51}

Jane looks up at the sound of the laughter. Her eyes are red from last night's tears. She's collecting her morning paper on a dew-covered lawn. She's in her dressing gown. Her house is across the road from the vacant block where the children are playing.

Paula bursts through her front door. She's dressed for work.

PAULA: [*calling across the street*] Kids … get in the car. [*Seeing Jane*] Hi.

> *Jane nods. She'd like to talk. But she knows Paula's in a rush.*

You okay?

JANE: Yeah.

> *Paula can tell she's not. The children emerge from the lantana.*

PAULA: [*to the kids*] Watch the road … [*To Jane*] I'll pop over after work.

> *Nik {follows Paula out. He's not long out of bed, still with the look of that morning's sex about him. He} carries the baby. {He kisses Paula goodbye. Jane looks over. The kiss lingers. She knows why Paula's running late.}*

> *Paula bundles the kids in the car. She drives away leaving Nik and Jane standing in their respective front yards.*

JANE: Do you want a coffee?

NIK: [*surprised by the invitation*] Yeah … sure.

SCENE 57 INT. THE KITCHEN – JANE'S HOUSE. MORNING.
{52}

Nik puts the baby down onto the kitchen floor to play and pulls up a stool at the kitchen bench as Jane prepares the coffee.

NIK: Pete was over last night.

JANE: How is he?

NIK: Not good.

JANE: How's the job hunting?

> *Nik shrugs. It's obviously not going well.*

Are you guys alright for money?

NIK: [*defensively*] Yeah.

JANE: You know if you needed some, or anything …

NIK: No …

JANE: I know Paula wouldn't take it …

NIK: She's doing extra shifts.

JANE: But if there's a bill or something that you need to clear …

NIK: It's fine.

JANE: Well, the offer's there.

> {*As she turns to fill the kettle her gown falls open revealing a glimpse of her breast. She feels Nik's gaze and hesitates for the briefest of moments before she pulls her gown closed, just as Nik hesitates for the briefest of moments before he turns his eyes away. The moment of sexual tension surprises them both.*}

SCENE 58 INT. THE BEDROOM – VALERIE AND JOHN'S HOUSE. MORNING.   {54}

(Note: in the finished film Scene 53 is the view from Valerie and John's house of the water and boats.) Valerie's eyes spring open like a startled bird. She blinks, comprehending a new day. She looks across to the empty space on John's side of the bed.

SCENE 59 INT. VALERIE AND JOHN'S HOUSE. MORNING.
{55}

Valerie enters. John is already dressed.

VALERIE: Why didn't you wake me?

JOHN: I thought you could do with the rest.

VALERIE: I'll just have a shower.

> *She moves away. John glances at her.*

JOHN: Actually, I've got an early start.

VALERIE: I'll only be ten minutes.

JOHN: Just take your own car.

VALERIE: Please … wait for me.

JOHN: [*sharply*] For Christ sake, {just drive yourself}.

> *Valerie is stung.*

I'm sorry.

VALERIE: No. You're absolutely right. Go on, you go. You'll beat the traffic.

> *John regrets having said anything.*

I've got a lecture to give tonight anyway.

JOHN: [*as he gathers his things*] So you'll be late?

> *Valerie is struck by the question. She nods as he goes.*

{SCENE 60 INT./EXT. JOHN'S CAR – THE COASTAL FREEWAY. MORNING.

Tight on John as he drives, his gaze fixed ahead. A trickle of blood runs from his nose and slowly crawls down his upper lip. He doesn't notice until it drips onto his white shirt. He puts his hand to his face and sees the blood. He's shocked.

He pulls the car over. He looks at the blood on his hands and his shirt. He finds a handkerchief and holds it to his nose. He stares ahead, his face and shirt bloodied.}

SCENE 61 INT. VALERIE'S OFFICE. DAY.   {56}

Tight on Sonja.

SONJA: I think he's having an affair.

> *Valerie remains silent – watching.*

He's distant, preoccupied … like he's holding something back.

VALERIE: What would you do if he was?

SONJA: I think I would leave.

VALERIE: Does that scare you?

SONJA: Yes. I don't know what it's like out there. I'm middle-aged. And I've got these two beautiful boys … But I like the lines around my eyes. I don't know if he does, but I do … I could survive. If I had to.

> *Valerie is silent, unsure whether she could.*

VALERIE: Do you still love him, Sonja?

> *We hold on Sonja as she hesitates.*

{SCENE 62 INT. A LIFT – VALERIE'S BUILDING. DAY.

Close on Sonja's face as she travels down in the lift. She looks at her reflection in the lift mirror. Her face is drawn. Her eyes are red. She puts her sunglasses on.

The lift reaches the ground floor. The doors open to reveal Patrick. He stands aside to allow Sonja to come out of the lift. She nods her thanks as she passes.

Patrick enters the lift and presses the button. The doors close.

SCENE 63 INT. VALERIE'S OFFICE. DAY.

Valerie sits at her desk. She looks at the phone.}

SCENE 64 INT. JOHN'S CAR – THE CITY LANEWAY. DAY.
{57}

John is parked in his car, staring ahead at the same forlorn corner of the lane as earlier. (Note: in the finished film his mobile rings. John does not respond.)

SCENE 65 INT. VALERIE'S OFFICE. DAY.   {58}

Valerie reaches for the phone; then her assistant Sarah's voice jars through the intercom.

SARAH: [*over the intercom*] Valerie … Patrick Phelan is here.

> *She looks at the door.*

SCENE 66 INT. VALERIE'S OFFICE. DAY.   {59}

Later. Valerie watches Patrick carefully. She senses a danger in him.

{PATRICK: I read your book, by the way.

> *Valerie feels the intrusion.*

Peter Phelps as Patrick in *Lantana*. (Photo: Elise Lockwood.)

I don't know how anyone could get over something like that.

VALERIE: Let's talk about you, Patrick.

> *Beat.*}

PATRICK: You don't like me, do you?

VALERIE: Is it important to you that I like you?

{PATRICK: I would have thought if you were going to help me ...

VALERIE: I don't agree. If I'm going to help you I need to remain as objective as I can. It's not about whether I like you or not.}

PATRICK: Would it make a difference if I was straight?

VALERIE: I'm not uncomfortable with your sexuality.

PATRICK: But is it a problem that I'm having an affair with a married man?

{VALERIE: I imagine it is for his wife.}

> *(Note: in the finished film Valerie tells him to stop making her the subject, stating that it is just another form of defence.) Beat – the tension between them is palpable.*

Let's look at your role in this triangle.

PATRICK: My role? I'm a respite from a marriage that's got too hard. He takes refuge in me, in what I offer him.

VALERIE: What do you offer him, Patrick?

PATRICK: Sex unencumbered by need.

> *Valerie is rigid with tension. The facade threatens to crack.*

He told me that making love to her is like trying to fill an empty well.

> *Valerie recoils inside.*

VALERIE: Why doesn't he leave her?

PATRICK: Good men don't know how to leave their wives.

VALERIE: Good men or cowardly men?

> *Hold.*

SCENE 67 INT. THE BATHROOM – VALERIE'S OFFICE. DAY.   {60}

Valerie bursts into the bathroom. Shaking. She reels back against the wall. She breathes the unease away.

SCENE 68 EXT. A CITY STREET. NIGHT.   {61}

Valerie makes her way along a crowded city footpath. The feeling is edgy. There's too many people caught in a heat wave. Something's got to give. She brushes up against a man as he passes. She wheels around.

VALERIE: What did you say?

> *The man turns and looks back. It's Pete.*

PETE: What?

VALERIE: You said something to me.

PETE: No.

> {*Valerie looks to the gathering crowd for help.*}

VALERIE: This man said something to me.

PETE: What are you talking about?

> *Pete looks to the crowd but he's only getting suspicious looks.*

VALERIE: You said something.

PETE: Bullshit.

VALERIE: I want your name.

> *He looks guilty, whether he is or not. He turns and moves through the crowd, wanting to get away.*

[*Yelling after him*] I want your name.

> *Pete disappears into the crowd. She looks around for help. She feels the humiliating scrutiny of strangers who have judged her as mad. She turns and keeps moving through the crowd.*

> *We pick up Pete, working his way through the sea of people. He keeps looking over his shoulder as though the trouble's going to follow him. He's on edge, clearly disturbed by the incident. Up ahead he sees the neon sign for a bar.*

SCENE 69 INT. A BAR. NIGHT.   {62}

Pete enters. He's still on edge. He makes his way to the bar.

PETE: Whisky and Coke …

> *He glances back at the door. He's shaken.*

LEON: [*out of view*] You right?

> *Pete looks. Leon is sitting on a stool along the bar. He nods him off, not wanting a conversation. Leon can see he's upset.*

Sure?

{PETE: You a good Samaritan or something?

LEON: No. Why, do I look like one?

> *Pete takes him in.*

PETE: No.} You look like a cop.

LEON: What?

PETE: Are you?

LEON: Well, yeah, I am, {but I never thought I looked like one.}

> *They hold on each other for a beat. {Then laugh.} The barman places Pete's drink before him. He takes a drink.*

PETE: This really fucking weird thing just happened.

> *Leon looks … ?*

I'm walking along the street just minding my own business and this woman … starts screaming at me.

LEON: What for?

PETE: Shit, I don't know. {She thought I said something to her. She just started screaming, wanting my name. And everybody's looking at me as though I'd done something wrong.}

LEON: Had you?

PETE: No. Jesus, I didn't touch her.

LEON: Fine.

PETE: I don't look for trouble.

LEON: It's finished.

{PETE: Yeah …

> *He gathers himself.*

I know. [*Suddenly embarrassed*] Shit. I'm sorry. I didn't mean to just come out with all that.

> *Leon tells him it's fine with a shrug.*

Can I buy you a drink?}

> *(Note: in the finished film Leon buys Pete the drink.)*

SCENE 70 INT. THE BEDROOM – NIK AND PAULA'S
HOUSE. NIGHT.   {64}

(Note: in the finished film Scene 63 is of the exterior of Nik and Paula's house.)
Paula and Hannah are on the bed rolling socks into pairs. Nik is in his jocks and
combing his wet hair at the mirror.

PAULA: Sharon said there's a booze bus on the freeway.

NIK: I'll take the back road home.

> *He pulls on his 'good jeans' and T-shirt.*

{PAULA: You could just get a taxi.

NIK: Oh, yeah, what's that going to cost?} Hannah, grab Dad's wallet
from the kitchen, would you?

> *Hannah dashes out of the room.*

She asked me in for coffee this morning.

PAULA: Who?

NIK: Jane.

PAULA: What for?

HANNAH: [*out of view*] I can't find it.

NIK: [*calling back*] On the fridge. [*Putting on shoes*] For a moment there I
thought she was trying to come onto me.

> *Paula laughs. Nik looks a little put out. The baby's crawling around on the*
> *floor. Paula lifts him up.*

PAULA: She's lonely, Nik, and you're bored. It's a lethal combination. Stay
away from her.

> *Nik looks peeved at Paula's easy dismissal of the threat.*

Come here.

> *Nik moves to her. She puts the baby on the bed beside them and pulls Nik*
> *down onto her and holds his face close to hers.*

You ever fuck with our marriage and I'll cut your balls off and hang
them on the line between your socks and your jocks. Got it?

NIK: Sure, babe.

> *They kiss. The baby's face is in there too, kissing Paula. Nik kisses the baby,*
> *gets off and heads toward the door.*

PAULA: Wake me up when you get home.

> *He looks back, smiles … She smiles, baby in her arms. He leaves the room. A moment's concern passes over her face.*

SCENE 71 INT. THE MALE TOILETS – THE BAR. NIGHT. {65}

Leon and Pete stand at the urinal. Leon's talking.

LEON: … And I'm running down this wall and suddenly this guy comes around the corner and [*thumping his spare hand against the wall*] smack …

> *Pete jumps a little and glances down at his shoes to check whether he's splashed himself.*

I run straight into him and just go for him. 'You fucking arsehole. Why don't you fucking look where you're going?'

PETE: [*zipping up*] But it was your fault.

LEON: Yeah, I know. I don't know where it's coming from but it's like some button's been pushed and I'm going for him. [*Zipping up and turning away*] And then I notice he's cowering …

PETE: [*washing his hands*] Yeah?

LEON: [*waiting for the tap*] And he's got blood all over his face. I've broken his fucking nose.

PETE: Shit.

> *He dries his hands as Leon washes his.*

LEON: When he gets up he starts to walk away. And then it happens, he breaks down.

> *Pete watches Leon, intrigued by the story.*

He starts to cry.

PETE: What for?

> *Leon looks at him.*

LEON: I don't know. I mean, what makes a man cry like that?

> *We sense that Pete knows the answer, not being too far from the experience himself.*

PETE: A lot of things.

> *Leon shrugs: maybe.*

So what'd you do?

LEON: Well … I held him … I just held him … but the whole time I'm
thinking … 'Stop being such a weak prick; pull yourself together, the
rest of us have to'.

Hold on Leon a moment, Pete looking at him.

PETE: Yeah … but don't you just want to fucking ball sometimes?

A beat on Leon, the whisky and emotion swimming around inside.

LEON: Yeah … but you don't, do you?

Leon leaves the toilets. Pete lingers a moment then follows.

SCENE 72 INT. LEON AND SONJA'S HOUSE. NIGHT.

{67, 68}

*(Note: in the finished film Scene 66 is the exterior of Leon and Sonja's house, with the
city visible over rooftops.) Leon comes through the front door. Dylan is on the couch
watching TV. There are empty take-away food packets on the table.*

LEON: [*moving through*] Hi.

DYLAN: We ordered you food. But we ate it.

Leon smirks as he starts to remove his tie.

LEON: Mum out?

DYLAN: Dancing.

*He checks his watch. He's a little annoyed. He moves into the hall. Music is
coming from Sam's room. The door is closed. Leon sniffs. He knows the smell.
He marches down the hall and goes to open the door. It's locked.*

LEON: Sam … open the fucking door.

*Leon waits, then shoulders the door open. The lock comes away. Sam's scrambling
to conceal his joint but the smoke lingers.*

What the fuck … Sam!

Leon is dumbfounded.

I'm a cop for Christ sake.

SAM: Oh, right, so you can get the good stuff.

*Leon instinctively moves to thump him but pulls back. Dylan appears at the
door.*

Anthony LaPaglia as Leon and Glenn Robbins as Pete in *Lantana*. (Photo: Elise Lockwood.)

DYLAN: What's going on?

LEON: Your brother's being an idiot.

DYLAN: So what's new?

LEON: Did you know about this?

> *Dylan's silence suggests he did.*

Have you tried it as well?

> *Dylan shakes his head. Leon turns on Sam.*

You ever give this shit to your brother and I'll belt your arse, sixteen years old or not.

> *Leon starts emptying drawers.*

Where's your stash?

SAM: This is all I've got.

LEON: {Don't fucking lie to me, Sam.}

> *Sam looks genuinely afraid. He reaches under his pillow and takes out a small bag of dope. Leon confiscates it.*

You're grounded {and if I ever find this stuff in the house again I swear boy I will drag you down to the station and show you where you're headed.}

> *He leaves. Sam's eyes smart with tears.*

SCENE 73 INT. A LATIN DANCE CLUB. NIGHT. {73}

The club is wild, the dancing hot. A Latin band is playing. Sonja is dancing the salsa with Jose, a handsome young Latino. She's enjoying herself, feeling good.

JOSE: You're a very beautiful woman, Sonja.

> *Sonja smiles, a little embarrassed. Nobody's told her that for a while. Jose moves in close and whispers in her ear.*

I'd like to fuck with you.

> *Sonja steps back, caught between being stunned and flattered. The sea of dancing moving around her.*

> *Leon enters, moving through the crowd, scanning the room. He's prickly, feeling out of place. He reaches the safety of the bar.*

LEON: A whisky.

> *He sees Sonja on the dance floor. He watches as she extricates herself from the amorous Jose and moves off the floor. She sees him. She suddenly feels self-conscious. She makes her way toward him. He doesn't take his eyes off her. He softens. We sense forgiveness from them both. She reaches him.*

SONJA: Hi.

LEON: You look like you're having a good time.

SONJA: I am.

LEON: Yeah. You're out enjoying yourself while our son's at home smoking dope.

SONJA: I know. I told him if he was going to do it, then to do it at home where at least we can control it.

LEON: Why didn't you tell me?

SONJA: You haven't been around much lately.

LEON: I'm not having drugs in the house, Sonja.

SONJA: Banning it isn't going to solve the problem.

LEON: What are you doing here, Sonja? Most of these guys aren't much older than Sam.

> *He regrets it as soon as he's said it. He sees the hurt in her face. She stares at him, then turns and walks back toward the dancing.*

{[*Apologetically*] Sonja … [*Under his breath*] Shit.}

> *She starts to move to the music. Age is no barrier when you know how to move. A number of young men engage her in dance, clearly appreciating her. (Note: in the finished film Sonja joins Jose, and whispers into his ear.)*

> *Leon watches the sweat, the youth, the virility, all the things he's losing. He turns away and makes his way out of the bar.*

SCENE 74 INT./EXT. VALERIE'S CAR – THE COASTAL FREEWAY. NIGHT.   {69}

Valerie's car speeds along the freeway past towering limestone cliffs. Up ahead she sees the exit off the freeway. It's like an entrance to a dark tunnel. She turns off. The car disappears into darkness.

SCENE 75 INT./EXT. VALERIE'S CAR – THE RIDGE ROAD. NIGHT.   {70}

The road is badly lit. The headlights cut a tunnel of light through thick bush. Valerie focuses on the patch of road ahead. She's driving fast. Ahead there's a tree. It would be easy not to take the bend. She closes her eyes.

SCENE 76 EXT. THE RIDGE ROAD. NIGHT.   {71}

The car brakes, slides through the rough taking out a road post and stops before impact. It rocks to stillness. It's quiet and dark. Only the headlights illuminate the thick bush before her.

SCENE 77 INT./EXT. VALERIE'S CAR – THE RIDGE ROAD. NIGHT.   {72}

Valerie breathes the shock of it away. She calms. She rests her head on the steering wheel. She summons herself. She tries to start the engine. It doesn't turn over. She tries again. And again. Nothing.

She reaches for her handbag and grabs her mobile phone. She switches it on and dials. It doesn't respond. The batteries are flat. She looks outside the window. It's black. (Note: in the finished film Valerie gathers together her belongings from the car and starts to walk.)

SCENE 78 INT./EXT. JOSE'S CAR – A STREET. NIGHT.   {74}

Jose and Sonja are kissing in the front seat of his car. He's coming on hard, Sonja's trying to come up for air. His hand slides along her stockinged leg and beneath her skirt.

SONJA: Wait …

> *He doesn't. He's burning for it.*

I thought we'd go back to your house.

JOSE: We can't. My mother.

> *Sonja baulks; she hadn't imagined him with a mother. Jose kisses her neck, his hand pushes up between her legs. We see Sonja's feet stretch and one black leather shoe slip off a foot.*

> *Jose's hand slips to the side of the seat and releases it back, a well-practised move. Sonja's eyes widen as she goes back.*

> *Jose wrestles with his belt and fly. He's pushing his pants down and her skirt up. Foreplay seems to be over.*

SONJA: Slow down …

> *Jose ignores her, becoming insistent.*

[*More firmly*] Get off.

> *He's obviously trying to commence intercourse as quick as he can.*

[*Shoving*] I said, get off.

JOSE: What's wrong?

> *Sonja reaches for her shoe.*

SONJA: I'm sorry … this … [*'was a bad idea.'*]

> *She opens the door and gets out. Jose yells as he starts the car.*

JOSE: Fucking uptight bitch …

> *He pulls away, leaving Sonja standing in the street holding one shoe. She watches the car go, feeling shaken and a little stupid.*

SCENE 79 EXT. THE RIDGE ROAD. NIGHT.   {75*}

Tight on Valerie's black leather shoes as she paces along the edge of the road. Up ahead she sees the dim lights of a phone box outside a disused service station.

SCENE 80 EXT. A DISUSED SERVICE STATION. NIGHT. {75*}

Valerie approaches the service station. It's full of menace in the dark. She moves toward the phone box.

SCENE 81 INT./EXT. THE PHONE BOX – THE DISUSED
SERVICE STATION. NIGHT.   {76}

Valerie enters the phone box. Graffiti adorns the walls. The phone books have long been stolen. The emergency numbers have been torn from the walls. She empties the change from her purse. Her fingers search for the right coin. She inserts it and dials.

SCENE 82 INT. VALERIE AND JOHN'S HOUSE. NIGHT. {77}

Waves can be heard on the beach below. The phone rings in the darkened interior. The answering machine clicks on. Valerie's voice falls into the empty room.

VALERIE: [*voice over, on the answering machine*] John … it's Valerie. Are you there?

SCENE 83 INT./EXT. THE PHONE BOX – THE DISUSED
SERVICE STATION. NIGHT.   {78}

Valerie is on the phone.

VALERIE: I've had an accident. I can't get the car started. I'm on the back road. I just wanted to get home … I'll try your mobile.

{SCENE 84 EXT. THE PHONE BOX – THE DISUSED
SERVICE STATION. NIGHT.

A wide shot reveals Valerie encased in the single light of the phone box. We see her insert another coin and dial again. She waits. Obviously John does not answer his mobile. She hangs up and stares out into darkness.}

SCENE 85 INT./EXT. THE PHONE BOX – THE DISUSED
SERVICE STATION. NIGHT.   {79, 80, 81}

(Note: in the finished film this scene cuts between John and Valerie's house with the answering machine and Valerie in the phone box.) Valerie inserts another coin. She

Barbara Hershey as Valerie in *Lantana*. (Photo: Elise Lockwood.)

waits. She closes her eyes against the reality of the answering machine. She waits for the message to play through.

VALERIE: I called road service, John. They said there'll be a ninety-minute wait. Where are you? You didn't say you were going to be late ... I can't stand this. Please ... I need you, John.

SCENE 86 INT./EXT. THE PHONE BOX – THE DISUSED SERVICE STATION. NIGHT.   {82*}

Later. Valerie looks at the coins remaining. Only enough for one more call. She inserts the last coin and dials. Close on her face, the phone at her mouth.

VALERIE: John ...

   She hesitates, cautious.

There's a man ... Patrick ... He's a client, John ... I don't understand this ... I don't understand us any more ...

   There is the glow of an approaching car. Valerie's head slowly turns toward it. She's numb with emotion, almost drunk with it. Her eyes focus on the lights and then a glimmer of hope.

SCENE 87 INT. VALERIE AND JOHN'S HOUSE. NIGHT.
                                                                         {82*}

(Note: in the finished film this scene takes place in the phone box.) {*The house is in darkness. A photo of Eleanor stares out into the shadows.*}

VALERIE: {[*voice over, on the answering machine*]} There's lights. There's a car coming. I'll wave it down, John ... Wait for me. We'll talk when I get home.

SCENE 88 INT./EXT. THE PHONE BOX – THE DISUSED SERVICE STATION. NIGHT.   {82*}

Valerie hesitates before hanging up.

VALERIE: I love you.

   She hangs up.

SCENE 89 EXT. THE PHONE BOX – THE DISUSED SERVICE STATION. NIGHT.   {83, 84}

Valerie comes out of the phone box. She moves to the side of the road and stares ahead at the approaching headlights.

She's caught in the glow of light. The wind catches her hair, she holds it back. She raises her hand in the air as we move toward her.

Dissolve to:

{SCENE 90 EXT. THE VACANT BLOCK. NIGHT.

The glow of approaching headlights through entangled lantana – Nik's ute pulls up in the front yard.}

SCENE 91 INT. THE MAIN BEDROOM – JANE'S HOUSE. NIGHT.   {85}

Tight on Jane's eyes open in the darkness. She's lying in bed; a stifling wind billows the curtains. She turns toward the window hearing the engine of a car. She moves to the window and sees that it's Nik returning from the pub. She's about to turn away when she sees him get out of the car with something in his hand. She can't make it out.

She watches him cross the road, hesitate a moment and then throw whatever it is into the vacant block. It strikes her as odd. She turns and moves away from the window.

Fade to black.

SCENE 92 EXT. THE SIDE OF THE ROAD. MORNING.   {86, 87, 88}

Fade up. Early morning. A bright new day. A bird's-eye view of Valerie's car. It sits at the side of the road. Abandoned. Widen to reveal police cars, search vehicles, the place is swarming.

Leon pulls up and gets out of his car. He takes in the scene. He looks dishevelled, hung over.

{CLAUDIA: [*approaching*] You look like shit.

    He warns her off with a look.}

LEON: What have we got?

    They move toward Valerie's car as Claudia fills him in.

CLAUDIA: Locals get a call about one a.m. from the husband. He gets home late. His wife's not there. She's left messages on the answering machine. She's run off the road. She's making calls from a phone box about two Ks down the road.

    Leon checks the scene. There are skid marks coming off the road.

The last call says she can see a car coming, she's going to wave it down and get a lift home. She never makes it.

    He looks around; there's a wall of twisted lantana on either side of the road. It looks impenetrable.

LEON: Fifty bucks it's the husband.

CLAUDIA: You're on.

SCENE 93 EXT. THE FRONT DOOR – VALERIE AND JOHN'S HOUSE. MORNING.   {89}

Leon and Claudia stand at the front door. The door opens to reveal John.

LEON: Mr Somers?

JOHN: No. Knox. My wife's name is Somers. My name is John Knox.

LEON: I'm Detective Sergeant Leon Zat. This is my colleague Senior Constable Claudia Weis.

    John shakes both their hands.

JOHN: You better come in.

SCENE 94 INT. VALERIE AND JOHN'S HOUSE. MORNING.
{90}

Leon and Claudia follow John inside. Claudia takes the place in.

LEON: Your wife's car has been located, Mr Knox.

    John looks at Leon, hoping for some word.

It looks as if she's run off the road. There's a phone box about two kilometres further along.

JOHN: Should I go there?

LEON: We've begun a search of the immediate area but if she has accepted a lift from somebody then it's unlikely she'll be there.

Claudia notices the photo of Eleanor; it's familiar.

Can I ask you a few questions, Mr Knox?

JOHN: I've been through it all.

LEON: I'm sorry to put you to any more trouble. But can you tell me what happened last night?

John looks bewildered, exhausted.

JOHN: I got home around midnight. Her car wasn't here. I came in and checked the machine. She'd been calling for about an hour. The last message said there was a car coming and she was going to wave it down.

LEON: So then you phoned the police.

JOHN: I waited for about twenty minutes. That's how long it should have taken for her to get home.

Leon's curious, his cop radar buzzing.

LEON: So it was about twenty past twelve?

JOHN: Yes, I think so. [*Annoyed*] I don't know.

CLAUDIA: Do you have a photo of your wife?

John nods. He opens a drawer to reveal the photo. He hands it to Claudia. She takes a look and passes it to Leon.

LEON: [*looking at the photo*] How was she yesterday?

John hesitates.

JOHN: Fine.

LEON: Nothing troubling her?

JOHN: [*tense*] No ... Why?

LEON: I'm just trying to get a sense of your wife's emotional state.

JOHN: Right now, I'd say her emotional state was pretty bad, wouldn't you? I'm going out of my mind here.

LEON: I can imagine.

JOHN: What can you imagine? Are you married?

Leon nods, uncomfortable.

If your wife got into a car with a stranger, some man let's assume, if she got into his car late at night and didn't come home, what would you imagine?

LEON: That right now I'd be close to going mad.

JOHN: Yes.

Beat.

{CLAUDIA: Is there somebody you could call? Somebody that could come over here, maybe?

He shakes his head.

[*Indicating the photo*] Your daughter?

JOHN: She died.

It dawns on Claudia.

CLAUDIA: Eleanor.

John is silent. Leon looks to Claudia for an explanation.

Eleanor Knox. She was ...

JOHN: Murdered ... She was murdered.

A beat.

CLAUDIA: Mr Knox's wife has written a book about it.

He looks at John, not without sympathy.

LEON: Yeah ... I remember the case...} We'll need to take the tape with us.

John hesitates, then ejects the tape and hands it to Leon. His hand is shaking.

JOHN: She ...

It's difficult.

It's private.

LEON: In what sense?

John meets Leon's eye, irritated.

JOHN: She didn't imagine anyone else would listen to it.

Leon nods, matter of fact.

LEON: I'll make sure it's returned.

SCENE 95 INT. NIK AND PAULA'S HOUSE. MORNING. {91}

Paula's dressed for work. The kitchen's a mess. She's in a rush. The baby's in the high chair. The older kids are eating their breakfast. Nik comes in. He has scratches on his face.

Paula looks across at him as he sits and starts to feed the baby.

PAULA: You didn't wake me up last night.

NIK: Got home a bit late.

PAULA: What's with the face?

NIK: I fell over.

PAULA: Were you pissed?

NIK: Yeah, a little.

> *Paula grabs her bag.*

PAULA: Come on, kids.

> *Hannah and George get up from the table and kiss Nik and the baby goodbye. Paula notices that Nik holds Hannah tight for a moment, the way a parent does when they're feeling vulnerable.*

SCENE 96 EXT. JANE'S HOUSE AND NIK AND PAULA'S HOUSE. MORNING.   {92}

Jane is returning from a jog as Paula and the kids emerge from the house in the usual rush.

JANE: Hi.

> *Paula doesn't want to get caught up in a conversation.*

[*Casually*] Nik got in late last night.

PAULA: Haven't you got anything better to do than spy on your neighbours? Get in the car, kids.

> *Jane is taken aback. Paula gets into the car and starts the engine.*

JANE: Paula … ?

PAULA: Look … don't have Nik in for coffee while I'm not here.

> *Jane is shocked. Paula reverses the car out of the drive. Jane looks across at Paula's house. She's mortified.*

{SCENE 97 INT. LEON'S DESK – THE POLICE STATION. DAY.

Leon is at his desk listening to the tape.

VALERIE: [*voice over, on tape*] John … There's a man … Patrick … He's a client, John … I don't understand this … I don't understand us any more … There's lights. There's a car coming. I'll wave it down, John … Wait for me. We'll talk when I get home … I love you.

> *Claudia approaches, scanning a file. Leon presses 'Stop'.*

CLAUDIA: Eleanor Knox. Twelve. The usual catastrophe. Bound, raped and strangled. Body dumped in a lane.

> *Leon takes it in.*

LEON: Twelve … I hate this job, Claudia.
CLAUDIA: No, you don't.}

SCENE 98 INT. VALERIE'S OFFICE. DAY.   {93}

Sarah leads Leon in. She points to a book on the desk.

SARAH: That's the appointment book. All her notes and session tapes are kept in the filing cabinet.

> *Leon scans the book.*

{LEON: How well do you know her, Sarah?
SARAH: I've worked for her for about four years.}
LEON: Do you think she'd ever get into a car with somebody she didn't know.
SARAH: No, not after what happened to her daughter.

> *Leon's finger stops at the name 'Patrick Phelan'.*

LEON: Could you print me out a list of her current clients, with addresses?
SARAH: Is that ethical?
LEON: Probably not.

> *Sarah nods then leaves. Leon notices the tape recorder still sitting on the table. He presses 'Eject'. Removes the tape. It is titled with the date and Patrick's name. He slips the tape into his pocket.*

He moves to the filing cabinet and opens the drawer. His fingers search the files until he comes across one headed with his own wife's name. He's stunned. He opens it, glances at the door, then removes the tapes.

SCENE 99 INT. THE LOUNGE ROOM – JANE'S HOUSE. DAY.   {94}

Jane is watching out the window as she sees Nik leaving his house with the baby in the pram. She watches him look over to the vacant block as he passes the house.

SCENE 100 EXT. JANE'S HOUSE. DAY.   {95}

Jane emerges from the house. She checks the street and sees that it's empty. She looks across to the vacant block. She crosses the road toward it.

SCENE 101 EXT. THE VACANT BLOCK. DAY.   {96}

Jane moves cautiously through the thick foliage of lantana, her eyes poring over the ground, looking for whatever Nik threw.

SCENE 102 EXT. JANE'S STREET. DAY.   {97*}

Nik is walking along the street pushing the pram. The baby is asleep. He reaches for his pack of cigarettes. They're not there. He pats his pockets, then realises he's forgotten them. He turns and heads back toward the house.

SCENE 103 EXT. THE VACANT BLOCK. DAY.   {97*}

(Note: in the finished film Jane sees Nik returning for his pack of cigarettes and ducks.) Jane moves through the lantana. It gets thicker and more twisted the deeper she goes. It's hot. Insects buzz in her face. She scratches her arm on a thorn. Then she sees it. A woman's shoe lying on the ground, black leather.

She stares at it, too afraid to move. She looks back and sees Nik coming back down the street. She freezes.

Across the road Nik stops outside his house and looks across at the vacant block. He hesitates, deciding what to do. He leaves the baby in the pram and crosses the road.

Jane sees him coming. She reaches down for the shoe. It's just out of reach. Nik is approaching. He's reached the block. She reaches the shoe and then conceals herself within the lantana as best she can. She hardly moves as Nik passes perilously close. She watches him through the foliage as his eyes scan the ground, looking for the shoe.

Jane holds it tightly to her chest. She presses her body further into the lantana. A thorn pricks her cheek. She winces silently with the pain. A trickle of blood runs down her cheek.

Suddenly there's a cry from the baby. Nik looks back, then glances once more around the ground. But the baby's cry is insistent. He turns away and moves back to the baby.

Jane crouches, rigid with fear.

SCENE 104 EXT. LEON'S CAR – A DISUSED INDUSTRIAL SITE. DAY.   {98*}

The car is parked. Rusting hulks of steel litter the dustbowl site.
SONJA: [*voice over, on tape*] I could survive … If I had to.

SCENE 105 INT./EXT. LEON'S CAR – A DISUSED INDUSTRIAL SITE. DAY.   {98*}

Leon is sitting in his car, listening to Sonja's tape.
VALERIE: [*voice over, on tape*] Do you still love him, Sonja?

> *Leon tenses. Sonja hesitates before answering. He doesn't want to hear it. He presses 'Stop' before she answers. He sits in silence.*

Rachael Blake as Jane in *Lantana*. (Photo: Elise Lockwood.)

SCENE 106 INT. THE KITCHEN – LEON AND SONJA'S HOUSE. EVENING. {99}

The television news is on in the background. Sonja is preparing dinner. Dylan is at the kitchen table doing homework.

NEWSREADER: [*over the TV*] Police are inquiring into the disappearance of a woman ...

> *Sonja glances up at the TV. Valerie's photograph fills the screen. She stares at us, a haunting portrait.*

[*Over the TV*] Psychiatrist and writer Valerie Somers was last seen on Friday night.

> *Sonja stares at the screen, deeply shocked. Dylan looks up and sees his mother's face. He looks at the TV screen.*

SCENE 107 INT. NIK AND PAULA'S HOUSE. EVENING. {100}

Nik is lying on the couch playing with the baby on his lap. George drives toy cars through a block construction on the floor. Through the door to the kitchen we can see Hannah working at the table and Paula preparing dinner. The news is on the television, showing footage of police searching through lantana undergrowth. Nik sits up and looks.

NEWSREADER: [*over the TV*] Her car was found abandoned along the lower Ridge Road. It is believed that she may have accepted a lift from a passing motorist around twelve p.m.

> *Paula comes through from the kitchen and looks at the TV screen.*

[*Over the TV*] Police are appealing to the public for information ...

{PAULA: Ridge Road?

NIK: I took the freeway.

> *Nik stares at the screen.*}

SCENE 108 INT. JANE'S HOUSE. NIGHT. {101}

(Note: in the finished film the newsreader goes on to report the details of Valerie's recently completed book and details of Eleanor's murder.) Jane is kneeling in front of the TV. {On TV John sits talking to camera. He looks drawn and dazed by the occasion.

JOHN: *[over the TV]* I fear for my wife's safety and implore anyone with information, no matter how seemingly inconsequential, to contact the police …

> *Jane looks across at her dining-room table. The black shoe sits at the centre of the table on a sheet of newspaper.}*

SCENE 109 INT./EXT. LEON'S CAR – THE COASTAL FREEWAY. NIGHT. {102, 103}

The car speeds down the freeway. Leon is driving John home. The freeway exit looms before them. Leon slows and takes it. John looks across at him.

SCENE 110 EXT. THE RIDGE ROAD. NIGHT. {104}

Leon's car cuts through the wall of lantana on either side.

SCENE 111 INT./EXT. LEON'S CAR – THE RIDGE ROAD. NIGHT. {105}

The headlights pick out the figure of a woman at the side of the road. Her hand is raised in the air as if to flag them down. It's Valerie. {John freezes. Leon looks across, gauging his response.

LEON: It's a mock-up. We've put it there in case it jogs anyone's memory.

> *John is clearly on edge. Leon pulls the car over.}*

Rachael Blake as Jane in *Lantana*. (Photo: Elise Lockwood.)

SCENE 112 EXT. THE ROAD AND PHONE BOX. NIGHT.

{106}

Leon and John get out of the car. John approaches the dummy of his wife. It's disconcerting, almost mocking. The area is taped off. There's a marked police car parked at the site. Leon waves over to the officer inside. He flicks his headlights in response.

LEON: Why do you think she turned off the freeway?

JOHN: Some people say it's shorter.

LEON: Who's Patrick Phelan, John?

JOHN: I don't know. She mentioned she was having trouble with a client.

LEON: What sort of trouble?

JOHN: She didn't go into it. She doesn't usually talk about her clients.

LEON: Why not?

JOHN: It's unprofessional.

LEON: What, even between a husband and wife?

>   *John nods.*

I tell my wife everything …

>   *Leon realizes the untruth of what he just said.*

JOHN: That surprises me.

LEON: Why?

JOHN: Most men hold something back. {It's in our nature.}

>   *A beat on Leon. John looks over at the phone box.*

LEON: You're some kind of academic, aren't you?

JOHN: I'm Dean of Law. I studied at Harvard. That's where Valerie and I met. I don't understand why she would get into a car with a stranger.

LEON: Maybe she didn't. Maybe she knew him.

>   *John looks across. He senses the insinuation.*

Is everything alright in your marriage, John?

JOHN: Yes, it's fine. How's yours?

LEON: Up and down lately. Where were you on Friday night?

JOHN: Am I a suspect in my wife's disappearance?

LEON: Where were you, John?

JOHN: I was at work.

LEON: Is there somebody we can check that out with?

JOHN: No. I was alone. Nobody saw me.

John gives Leon a long look daring him to challenge it.

LEON: Nine times out of ten, when a wife goes missing the husband knows something about it.

JOHN: You're a prick.

Leon moves toward his car.

LEON: The constable will take you home.

Leon gets into his car. John watches him pull away.

SCENE 113 INT. THE POLICE STATION. NIGHT.   {108}

(Note: in the finished film Scene 107 is of Leon driving on the freeway, listening to the recordings of Patrick's appointments.) Leon enters. The place is deserted except for Claudia. She sits with a plastic cup of coffee reading Valerie's book.

LEON: Don't you have a home to go to?

CLAUDIA: Yes. Do you?

LEON: Found anything?

CLAUDIA: She dedicates the book to John. 'For teaching me to trust again.'

Leon sits across the desk from her.

{Phone room's had about twenty calls. Several report her involved in some incident on the street around ten p.m.

LEON: Any description?

CLAUDIA: They're being followed up. Doesn't sound like the husband, though.

LEON: The man's got something going on. He doesn't have an alibi for Friday night …}Have you listened to Phelan's tape?

She nods.

What do you think?

{CLAUDIA: She didn't like the man.

LEON: Do you blame her? … It's like he's warning her off or something … Or trying to let her know.

CLAUDIA: What?

LEON: That he's fucking her husband.
CLAUDIA: You're kidding.

> *Leon shrugs.}*

LEON: Go home. We've got an early start.
{CLAUDIA: Phelan?
LEON: First thing.}

> *Claudia starts to gather her things.*

Have you spoken to your mystery man yet?

> *She shrugs it off.*

CLAUDIA: He never came back.

> *A beat on Claudia – a glimpse of her loneliness. She waves it away as she heads out the door. Leon sits in the silence.*

SCENE 114 INT. LEON AND SONJA'S HOUSE. NIGHT.

{109}

Moonlight illuminates the room. Sonja lies in bed staring at the ceiling. The house is quiet. She hears the front door open. Leon appears at the bedroom door. He stands watching her.

SONJA: I'm not asleep.

> *He moves to the bed and sits on the edge.*

LEON: Have you seen the news?

> *She nods.*

SONJA: Will you find her?
LEON: It's not looking good.

> *Sonja is silent, thinking of Valerie's fate.*

I've seen her client list, Sonja.

> *Sonja doesn't say anything.*

Why didn't you tell me?
SONJA: It was private. Something I needed to do.
LEON: It wasn't long ago that private didn't exist between you and me.

> *They sit in the silence, estranged.*

SCENE 115 INT. THE KITCHEN – LEON AND SONJA'S HOUSE. NIGHT.   {110}

Leon sits at the kitchen table. He sips a shot glass of whisky. Sonja comes to the kitchen door. She's wearing Leon's pyjamas. She takes a glass from the cupboard and pours herself a splash of whisky. She sits at the table, opposite him. They sit in silence until Leon looks up at her.

LEON: I have to tell you something ...

> *Sonja waits. She doesn't look at him. She knows what's coming.*

I had an affair.

> *She doesn't say anything.*

I slept with the woman twice. I hurt her. And I hurt you. And I gained nothing.

SONJA: [*quiet, still*] Why?

> *He doesn't respond. She looks back at him, demanding it.*

LEON: I wanted to feel something. Something wrong ... Because I'm numb. Totally fucking numb.

> {*Sonja's grip on her glass tightens then she throws the whisky in his face. She gets up and walks out of the room. Leon sits at the table, his face a mask, dripping.*}

SCENE 116 EXT. LEON AND SONJA'S HOUSE. MORNING.
{111}

Establishing shot of the house in the morning.

SCENE 117. INT. THE LOUNGE ROOM – LEON AND SONJA'S HOUSE. MORNING.   {112}

Dylan passes through on his way to the kitchen. He sees a blanket and pillow scrunched on the couch. It's been slept on.

SCENE 118 INT. THE KITCHEN – LEON AND SONJA'S HOUSE. MORNING. {113}

Dylan comes into the kitchen and sees the heavy silence between his parents. Sam is already at the table. Leon is cleaning up.

DYLAN: Why'd you sleep on the couch?

LEON: I got home late. I didn't want to wake Mum up.

Sonja turns away and throws the dregs of her tea into the sink.

DYLAN: Are you fighting?

LEON: Yeah, a bit.

DYLAN: Why?

LEON: It's something we've got to sort out, alright?

Dylan looks at Sonja.

DYLAN: Are you alright, Mum?

Sam looks up from his breakfast. Sonja's been keeping it in but her son's concern brings her close to tears. She nods. Sam gets up from the table and slings his bag over his shoulder.

SAM: I'll be in the car.

Leon watches him stalk out of the room.

SONJA: Grab something to eat. We're running late.

Dylan grabs some fruit and follows Sam out. Sonja finishes wiping down the sink, then turns to leave.

LEON: So ... what? You don't want to deal with this? Is that how you're going to punish me?

She grabs her bag.

I fucked up, alright? People do.

SONJA: I don't. Jesus, Leon. It's so easy to go out and find someone. What's hard is not to.

She goes to move. He reaches out and takes her arm. She turns on him and flays him with her fists. He takes her blows until she turns away, shaking. They are silent as she settles. She moves toward the door. Leon needs reassurance.

LEON: We'll talk about it tonight, alright?

SONJA: I don't even know if I'm going to be here tonight.

SCENE 119 EXT. LEON AND SONJA'S HOUSE. DAY. {114}

{*Dylan and Sam are sitting in the car. Sam's door is suddenly yanked open.*

CLAUDIA: Get out of the car. You're under arrest for possession of marijuana.

SAM: [*scowling*] Very funny.

   Claudia closes the door and sticks her head through the window.

CLAUDIA: Don't worry, Sammy. It comes back when you're twenty.

SAM: What?

CLAUDIA: You're sense of humour.}

   She turns and heads toward the house to see Sonja come out the front door. Claudia can see the tightness in her face.

   Hi.

   It's awkward between them. They are fond of each other but Sonja knows that Claudia is Leon's friend first and foremost.

SONJA: Did you know about it?

   Claudia can't answer. It just confirms it. Sonja moves on, leaving Claudia feeling implicated in the mess.

SCENE 120 INT. THE KITCHEN – LEON AND SONJA'S HOUSE. MORNING.   {115}

Claudia comes to the door. Leon sits in stillness at the table. She can see the dread in his face.

CLAUDIA: You ready?

SCENE 121 EXT. PATRICK'S HOUSE. DAY.   {117*}

Leon's police car pulls up. Leon and Claudia get out of the car and move toward the house. Leon's moving fast, the professional and the private mixed up into a volatile emotional stew. Claudia can sense it.

CLAUDIA: You up to this?

Leon gives her a sharp look, then knocks hard on the door. He waits. He goes to knock again. Claudia puts her hand on his arm, slowing him a notch. The door is opened. Patrick's face peers out of the darkness.

SCENE 122 INT. PATRICK HOUSE. DAY.   {117*, 118}

Patrick leads Leon and Claudia in. The blinds are drawn.

LEON: We're investigating the disappearance of Valerie Somers, Mr Phelan. We're hoping you can help us.

{CLAUDIA: Do you have something against the sun?

PATRICK: Only before twelve.} I was out late.

LEON: Who with?

> *Claudia shoots Leon a glance. A beat on Patrick. He can feel the edge in Leon.*

PATRICK: A friend. Why?

{CLAUDIA: [*moving to the blind*] Do you mind?

> *He shakes his head. She opens the blind. Light floods the room.*

This is all fairly routine. We're speaking to anyone who saw Valerie on the day she disappeared.}

PATRICK: Do you know what's happened to her?

CLAUDIA: Not yet.

LEON: You had an appointment with her. Can you tell us how she was?

PATRICK: She seemed alright. I don't know.

LEON: How'd you get on with her?

> *Patrick hesitates. He's distracted. There's someone in his bedroom. Leon notices.*

PATRICK: Alright … She was my therapist.

> *Leon waits for more.*

We didn't end our last session on very good terms.

LEON: Yeah? Why's that?

PATRICK: We disagreed about something.

LEON: About this bloke you're seeing? This married guy.

> *Patrick tenses. Claudia looks at Leon, dismayed.*

PATRICK: How do you know about that?

LEON: She makes a recording of her sessions.

PATRICK: Yeah, but what's said in that room is confidential.

LEON: Under the circumstances …

PATRICK: That's my life.

{LEON: The woman's missing, Mr Phelan. We just want to find her.

PATRICK: I can't help you.}

LEON: Is somebody in your room?

> *Patrick's silence confirms it.*

Who is it, your boyfriend?

> *Patrick doesn't answer.*

Can you ask him to come out here?

PATRICK: He's got nothing to do with this.

> *Leon moves toward the bedroom door.*

What are you doing?

> *Patrick stands in his way. Leon manhandles him away.*

You don't have the right.

CLAUDIA: Leon …

> *Leon opens the door, expecting to see John. A man is sitting on the bed.*

PATRICK'S LOVER: Who the fuck are you?

> *Leon turns away to face Patrick.*

PATRICK: You finished?

{LEON: Look …

PATRICK: Get out …}

SCENE 123 EXT. PATRICK'S HOUSE. DAY.   {119}

Leon and Claudia move onto the footpath away from the house.

CLAUDIA: That went well.

> *Leon ignores it.*

Leon …

> *He stops, looks back, irritated.*

{You just fucked that up.

LEON: I know that.}

CLAUDIA: Your marriage is falling apart and so are you.

LEON: It's none of your business, Claudia.

CLAUDIA: Bullshit. If you can't do your job, it's my business.

LEON: If you've got a concern about how I'm handling this then bring it up at the station.

He heads toward the car. Claudia follows.

{SCENE 124 INT. THE BACKYARD – JANE'S HOUSE. DAY.

Jane is walking along a path through her back garden. She can hear Nik and the kids playing with a ball in their backyard.

She keeps glancing at the fence. They sound so close; just a few pickets away. She treads carefully, as though she doesn't want to be heard. She moves steadily toward her backdoor. Suddenly a ball bounces before her. She gasps with fright. She looks up. Nik is watching her, his head over the fence.

NIK: Did I scare you?

Jane shakes her head.

Can we have the ball?

Jane looks for the ball. She grabs it and throws it back over.}

SCENE 125 INT. JANE'S HOUSE. DAY.   {116}

(Note: in the finished film Jane watches Nik playing with his children from her window.) {*Jane comes in through the patio door.*} *She's tense. She doesn't know what to do. She moves to the phone. She checks a number on her fridge. She hesitates before dialling. It's not a call she wants to make. She dials.*

JANE: Pete … It's Jane … Can you come over?

{SCENE 126 INT./EXT. LEON'S CAR – TRAFFIC LIGHTS. DAY.

Leon pulls up at the lights. He looks across. Valerie stares at him from the poster for that morning's daily. Her blown-up photo sits under the headline 'Missing'. He looks away.}

SCENE 127 INT. THE KITCHEN – LEON AND SONJA'S HOUSE. DAY.   {122}

(Note: in the finished film Scene 121 Leon is driving.) Sam stacks the dishwasher while Dylan clears the table after dinner. The phone rings. Dylan takes the call as Sonja comes in into the room.

DYLAN: Hello … Hi, Dad.

    Sonja looks over.

SCENE 128 INT./EXT. LEON'S CAR. DAY.   {123}

The car is parked. Leon is on his mobile phone.

LEON: Can I talk to Mum, son?

SCENE 129 INT. THE KITCHEN – LEON AND SONJA'S HOUSE. DAY.   {124, 125}

Dylan holds out the phone. Sonja shakes her head.

DYLAN: Nuh. She's still pissed off with you.

SCENE 130 INT./EXT. LEON'S CAR. DAY.   {126}

Leon, on the phone.

LEON: Look, tell her … I'll be home soon.

SCENE 131 INT. THE KITCHEN – LEON AND SONJA'S HOUSE. DAY.   {127}

Dylan hangs up the phone. Sonja looks, waits.

DYLAN: He said to say that he's sorry, that he loves you and that he wants you to stop being angry with him.

> *Sonja smiles at Dylan's attempt. We hold on her.*

{What's he done, Mum?

SONJA: It's not up to me to tell you.

SAM: He's cheated on you, hasn't he?

> *Sonja doesn't say anything. The three of them stand in an uncertain silence. Then Dylan runs out of the room.*}

SCENE 132 EXT. THE CITY LANEWAY. DUSK.   {120}

John is standing in the darkened laneway – looking at the place his daughter was murdered. Everything is silent. He turns and starts to walk away leaving a ragged bunch of flowers marking the spot.

SCENE 133 EXT. VALERIE AND JOHN'S HOUSE. NIGHT.
{128}

John's car pulls up in the drive. He gets out. He's carrying a bottle in a liquor-store bag. He locks the car door and moves up the path to find Leon sitting on the front step. Leon looks up at him. They meet one another's eyes.

JOHN: You look ... bereft, Leon.

> *Leon smiles at the aptness of the description.*

LEON: Yeah ... The question is how come you don't?

> *John starts toward the door ...*

JOHN: Don't be deceived by appearances ...

> *He unlocks the front door.*

Do you drink whisky?

SCENE 134 INT. VALERIE AND JOHN'S HOUSE. NIGHT.

John pours whisky into two glasses. Leon is sitting.

{LEON: I need to know where you were on Friday night, John.

> *John places the glass of whisky before Leon.*

JOHN: Why? Why do you need to know?

LEON: Because} I think somebody has harmed your wife and I need to know if it was you.

JOHN: I didn't ... hurt Valerie.

> *(Note: in the finished film Leon questions John as to why Valerie was upset on the phone. John tells him that she was afraid of being alone, of him not being there for her. Leon asks John whether he is having an affair with a man, telling him that he thinks Valerie thought that was happening.)*

LEON: Then where were you?

> *John hesitates ... This is somewhere he doesn't want to go.*

JOHN: I left work late ... and stopped at the place where my daughter was killed. I go there sometimes. Valerie didn't know.

LEON: You didn't tell her?

> *He shakes his head.*

Why not?

JOHN: Because ... some things don't need to be understood.

> *Leon wants more.*

{Valerie would need to know. She's a therapist. She uses words to reveal the truth. I'm a lawyer. I use them to obscure it.}

LEON: Is that what you're doing now?

JOHN: It was something private. Something of my own.

> *John finishes his whisky.*

Can't you leave this alone?

LEON: No.

> *John pours himself another.*

So you say you were at the place your daughter was killed when your wife was in some phone box calling you for help.

Geoffrey Rush as John in *Lantana*. (Photo: Elise Lockwood)

JOHN: Yes.

LEON: Is there any reason why she would think you were involved with someone else?

JOHN: An affair?

LEON: If you want to call it that?

JOHN: Valerie believed all men were capable of betrayal.

LEON: Including you?

JOHN: Have you ever cheated on your wife?

Leon masks his discomfort.

LEON: No.

JOHN: Never desired another woman?

LEON: Of course.

JOHN: But you've never acted on that?

LEON: [*bare-faced*] No.

JOHN: Then you're a better man than I am.

A beat on Leon. He knows he is no better than John.

LEON: So you are seeing someone?

JOHN: No. There was someone … once. Someone I loved. And once it's happened you're never entirely believed again. Something is permanently broken; trust, I suppose.

{LEON: Why didn't you leave her?

JOHN: Our daughter was murdered.

He meets Leon's eye.

How do you leave a woman in that much pain?

Leon has no answer.}

What holds your marriage together, Leon? You've asked me to reveal myself. Now I'm asking you to do the same.

LEON: Loyalty … love … maybe habit … sometimes passion … our kids.

JOHN: Ours was held together by grief. That's all those bastards left us.

He sips his whisky. Waves crash on the beach below.

SCENE 135 INT. THE POLICE STATION. NIGHT.   {130, 131}

Leon walks through the station – a man with nowhere else to go. Claudia is fired up as she finds him.

CLAUDIA: Where the hell have you been?

> *Leon looks at her.*

We've had a call. A man saying his wife saw her neighbour throw a shoe into a vacant block on the night Valerie disappeared. She has the shoe. Black leather.

> *They start moving.*

LEON: Where we going?

> *Claudia checks her notepad.*

{CLAUDIA: Thirty-one Chelmsford St, Brookvale.

> *Leon stops dead. He knows the address.*}

SCENE 136 INT./EXT. LEON'S CAR – JANE'S HOUSE. NIGHT.   {132}

Leon's car pulls up. Leon looks at the house. There's a light shining on the verandah.

LEON: This could be ... tricky.

CLAUDIA: Why?

LEON: I know the woman.

> *Claudia looks across ... The look on Leon's face says it all.*

{CLAUDIA: [*getting out of the car*] It's times like this I'm glad I don't have a dick.}

SCENE 137 EXT. JANE'S HOUSE. NIGHT.   {133*}

Leon and Claudia get out. Leon scans the lantana-covered block opposite. He looks at the house. He's feeling edgy; he doesn't know which way this is going to go.

They move up the path to the front door. Claudia knocks. The door opens revealing Pete. He takes Leon in.

PETE: [*surprised*] Leon … We met the other night.

LEON: Yeah … How are you?

> *Claudia shoots Leon a glance.*

PETE: You better come in. My wife's pretty upset.

> *He leads them down the hall.*

SCENE 138 INT. JANE'S HOUSE. NIGHT.   {133*}

Valerie's shoe is still on the table. Jane is waiting, tense, as Pete leads Leon and Claudia into the room.

PETE: Jane.

> *She turns and sees Leon. Leon and Jane hold on each other.*

{LEON: It's bad luck to put a shoe on your table.

> *Jane starts looking for something.*

JANE: Where are my cigarettes? Pete?

PETE: [*passing her the packet*] Here.}

LEON: You know Mrs … ?

JANE: O'May. Jane O'May.

LEON: You shouldn't have touched the shoe.

JANE: Well, I did.

LEON: But you shouldn't have.

JANE: But I did. It's there. On my table. I touched it, alright?

> *Pete doesn't understand the animosity between them.*

CLAUDIA: [*to Pete*] Do you think we could have some coffee?

> *Pete nods. He exits to the kitchen.*

[*Following*] I'll give you a hand.

> *Jane's trying to light her cigarette but her hands are shaking. Leon takes the box of matches and strikes a match. She looks up into his face. It's a softer moment between them. He notices that she's wearing the pearl earrings. She lights the cigarette.*

LEON: You alright?

> *Jane draws hard and moves away. She's not alright.*

How do you want to handle this?

JANE: You're a policeman, aren't you? Do your job. I've never seen you before.

{SCENE 139 EXT. THE BACKYARD – NIK AND PAULA'S HOUSE. NIGHT.

Nik is tinkering with a car engine on blocks. Hannah appears at the back door, sleepy and in her pyjamas.

HANNAH: Dad.

Nik looks up.

Something's going on across the road.

He tightens. He's been waiting for something like this.}

SCENE 140 EXT. NIK AND PAULA'S HOUSE. NIGHT. {134}

Nik parts the curtain and looks across the road.

Police cars everywhere. Spotlights being erected. The vacant block is being taped off. A search squad is preparing.

He lets the curtain fall. He's thinking fast, trying not to let the panic sweep him away. He moves to the phone and dials.

NIK: Hello … Can I speak to Paula? It's Nik, her husband.

He looks at Hannah's face. She knows something's up. He has to look away. He's going to lose it.

[*Into the phone*] It's urgent. Well, tell her to call home as soon as she can.

He hangs up. There's a knock at the door. Nik looks startled. Hannah moves to answer the door.

Leave it … Get the boys up, Baby.

They knock again. Nik goes to the door and answers it. Claudia and a uniformed officer are standing on the doorstep.

CLAUDIA: Nik D'Amato?

NIK: My kids … I've got to find someone for my kids.

SCENE 141 INT. JANE'S HOUSE. NIGHT.   {135}

A gloved officer places Valerie's shoe into a plastic bag. Another police officer is taking a statement from Jane, who's sitting at the table.

Leon moves outside.

SCENE 142 EXT. JANE'S HOUSE. NIGHT.   {136, 137*}

{*Leon meets Claudia coming up the front path.*

CLAUDIA: He's trying to find someone to take his kids.

LEON: What about the mother?

CLAUDIA: She's at work.}

> *Nik comes out of his house escorted by the uniformed officer. He's carrying a bag and the baby. The baby's crying. Hannah and George are following dutifully behind. Hannah's holding George's hand. They each carry a pillow and a teddy. Claudia and Leon watch them as they come out of their yard and go into Jane's and Pete's yard.*

{Ah … Nik. What are you doing?

NIK: I'm taking them next door until Paula gets back.

CLAUDIA: Isn't there anyone else?

> *Nik shakes his head.} He glances briefly at Leon, recognising him. Leon turns away. Nik continues up the path. Pete comes to the door.*

NIK: You back, Pete?

PETE: Yeah.

NIK: How are you?

PETE: I'm okay.

NIK: I'm in trouble, mate.

> *George wanders past Pete into the house.*

Could you take the kids?

> *Pete hesitates.*

Just till Paula gets home.

SCENE 143 INT. JANE'S HOUSE. NIGHT.   {137*}

Jane's standing in the house out of sight. She can hear Nik's voice at the door. Suddenly George appears and looks up to her.

NIK: [*out of view*] I wouldn't ask if I didn't need the help.

> *Jane takes George's hand. She steps out into the hall.*

JANE: We'll take them.

> *Nik meets her eye. He knows she called the police but there's no blame.*

NIK: [*passing Pete the bag*] They've got some pyjamas and toothbrushes and a video and stuff in there.

> *Nik passes over the baby. Pete takes him. He's not used to it but we get the sense that he'd like to be. The baby starts to cry. Pete retreats into the house, reassuring him.*

> *Nik starts to leave. Hannah grabs his waist. He prises her off and pushes her toward the door.*

> *Hannah stands on the verandah and watches him move down the path to the waiting police car. She's crying. Jane comes and stands with her. She takes Hannah's hand. They watch Nik get into the car with Leon and Claudia.*

SCENE 144 INT. THE INTERVIEW ROOM – THE POLICE STATION. NIGHT.   {138}

Nik is sitting quietly at a table. Leon and Claudia are standing.

LEON: How'd you get the marks on your face, Nik?

NIK: I want to see my wife.

CLAUDIA: She's on her way.

LEON: Can you tell us where you were on Friday night?

NIK: I want to see Paula.

> *Leon leans down so that his face is close to Nik's.*

LEON: [*softly*] You're in deep shit, Nik. Your wife can't help you.

> *Nik meets his eye.*

NIK: I know you.

Leon pulls away.

LEON: I doubt it.

NIK: Yeah, I've seen you before.

> *Claudia looks to Leon, wondering what's going on. Leon's trying unsuccessfully to look comfortable.*

Next door with Jane.

> *Leon snaps. He grabs Nik and thrusts him back against the wall hard. He holds his face close to Nik's.*

SCENE 145 INT. THE WAITING ROOM – THE POLICE STATION. NIGHT. {139}

Paula is in full force. A uniformed policewoman is with her.

PAULA: My kids … Where are my bloody kids?

CLAUDIA: [*coming in the room*] They're with your neighbour.

{PAULA: What the hell does she know about kids?}

CLAUDIA: Calm down.

PAULA: {Fuck you.} I don't want to be calm.

> *Claudia remains sympathetic.*

CLAUDIA: Can I get you something?

PAULA: Yeah. You can get me my husband. You can get me the hell out of here.

SCENE 146 INT. THE INTERVIEW ROOM – THE POLICE STATION. NIGHT. {141}

(Note: in the finished film Scene 140 is of the exterior of the interview room.) Paula is sitting very still, alone in the room. The door opens. Leon and Claudia enter.

LEON: Hello Mrs D'Amato. I'm Detective Sergeant Zat. You've met Detective Constable Weis.

PAULA: I want to see Nik.

{LEON: A woman's gone missing.

PAULA: What's it got to do with me?}

LEON: Your husband's helping us with our inquiries.

{PAULA: It's eleven o'clock. Helping you with your inquiries bullshit. Now, what's going on?}

LEON: He was seen throwing a shoe into a vacant block.

PAULA: Who saw him?

LEON: A search was made of the block opposite your house.

PAULA: Yeah, I know the one. My kids play there. Every kid in the street plays there.

LEON: A shoe was found on that block.

> *She takes this in.*

It has been identified as belonging to Valerie Somers. She's been missing since Friday night.

> *Paula is silent as it sinks in. Things adding up to an answer she doesn't want to believe.*

SCENE 147 INT. THE INTERVIEW ROOM – THE POLICE STATION. NIGHT.   {142}

Nik is guarded by a uniformed officer. He's pacing the room like an animal. He kicks over a chair.

NIK: [*yelling*] Paula!

SCENE 148 INT. THE FOYER – THE POLICE STATION. NIGHT.   {143}

Paula is on the phone, her voice weak with fear.

PAULA: Jane … it's Paula.

SCENE 149 INT. JANE'S HOUSE. NIGHT.   {144}

Jane is on the phone.

JANE: The kids are fine, Paula.

SCENE 150 INT. THE FOYER – THE POLICE STATION.
NIGHT.   {145}

PAULA: [*into the phone*] Is Hannah awake? Maybe I could just talk to Hannah.

SCENE 151 INT. JANE'S HOUSE. NIGHT.   {146}

JANE: [*into the phone*] She's asleep, Paula. They're all asleep.

SCENE 152 INT. THE FOYER – THE POLICE STATION.
NIGHT.   {147}

Paula's on the verge of breaking down.

PAULA: [*into the phone*] Sorry about this, Jane. I'm sorry.

    She's crying now.

  Nik's in trouble. They won't let me see him. I don't know what to do.

SCENE 153 INT. JANE'S HOUSE. NIGHT.
                                             {148, 149, 150, 151, 152}

(Note: in the finished film this scene cuts between Paula at the police station and Jane on the couch. Paula thanks Jane.) Jane is now crying too. Pete watches her nearby.

PAULA: [*voice over, on the phone*] I'll get there as soon as I can.

JANE: It's okay, Paula. It's okay. The kids are safe here.

    Jane replaces the receiver.

PETE: Does she know you called the cops?

    Jane shakes her head.

SCENE 154 INT. THE CORRIDOR – THE POLICE STATION.
NIGHT.   {153}

Leon leads Paula down the corridor to a door. Paula stands a moment to summon her strength.

SCENE 155 INT. THE INTERVIEW ROOM – THE POLICE STATION. NIGHT.   {154}

Nik hears the door open. He doesn't look up. Leon leads Paula into the room. They are silent for a moment. Paula can't look at him; she's too scared by what she'll see in his face.

Nik looks up. His eyes are wet. He's not a man used to crying; it's very painful for them both.

PAULA: They say you hurt some woman, Nik.

> *Leon's watching, closely gauging his response.*

NIK: I didn't, babe. I didn't touch her.

> *Paula's very still. That's all it takes. His word. For Paula there is no question about it. Nik's innocent. She moves to him and wraps her arms around him. He breaks down and cries. Paula looks up at Leon.*

{PAULA: You heard him … He didn't do it.}

> *A beat on Leon – watching. He's moved by the intensity of their commitment to each other.*

{LEON: Yeah, well, I'm going to need more than your word, I'm sorry.}

SCENE 156 INT. THE MAIN BEDROOM – JANE'S HOUSE. NIGHT.   {155}

Jane is lying in bed. Pete is lying beside her, looking close into her face. He reaches out, strokes her cheek. She pulls away slightly, involuntarily. Pete leans over and kisses her lightly.

JANE: Don't … Not yet.

> *Hannah's at the door watching. Jane sits up with a start.*

What is it, Hannah?
HANNAH: The baby's sick.

> *Jane's up in a flash and heading out of the room.*

SCENE 157 INT. THE SECOND BEDROOM – JANE'S
HOUSE. NIGHT.   {156}

Jane is bent over the baby. Pete comes in, doing up his gown.

JANE: He's burning up.

> *They look at each other. They've never had much to do with kids.*

Get some water. A flannel. A wet flannel.

> *Pete dashes out.*

HANNAH: He needs Panadol.

JANE: What? [*Calling*] Pete … Panadol. Get Panadol.

> *She strokes the baby, trying to soothe him.*

Poor baby.

> *Pete comes in with Panadol, trying to read the packet.*

PETE: Is this alright for babies?

JANE: I don't know. Maybe half.

HANNAH: Baby Panadol.

> *They both look at Hannah.*

JANE: You'll have to go to a chemist.

HANNAH: There's some in our house. {In the drawer near Mum's bed.}

SCENE 158 INT. NIK AND PAULA'S HOUSE. NIGHT.   {157}

Jane comes in through the back door. She moves rapidly through the house. Dishes in the sink. Toys on the floor. Garbage overflowing.

She moves into the hall. Piles of dirty clothes on the floor. She curses as she kicks something on the way through.

{*She moves into Paula and Nik's bedroom. The bed is not made. The sheets are twisted in bundles. Paula's scrunched-up uniform is at the end of the bed. Nik's underwear hangs on a chair. Everything is so personal, so intimate.*

She opens the bedside drawer and rummages through papers, condoms, sleeping tabs, a little bag of dope. She finds the baby Panadol.

She turns to go. Then stops still just for a moment. She looks around the room at all the mess and intimate details in Nik and Paula's life. She picks up Paula's uniform and folds it neatly over the back of a chair.}

SCENE 159 INT. THE INTERVIEW ROOM – THE POLICE STATION. NIGHT. {158}

Tight on Nik. A tape recorder is running.

NIK: I'd met some mates for a drink. We used to work together and it's just something we keep up.

>   *Leon and Claudia are listening.*

We drank more than we should've so I took the back road home. The police don't patrol it. It must have been about a quarter to twelve.

SCENE 160 INT./EXT. NIK'S CAR – THE RIDGE ROAD. NIGHT. {159*}

Flashback. Nik's driving. Up ahead he sees the figure of a woman standing at the side of the road. It's Valerie. She raises her hand.

NIK: [*voice over*] And I see this woman standing at the side of the road.

SCENE 161 INT. THE INTERVIEW ROOM – THE POLICE STATION. NIGHT. {159*}

NIK: I don't want to stop. It's late and I think Paula will be getting worried. But what do I do? The woman needs help. So I pull over.

SCENE 162 INT./EXT. NIK'S CAR – THE RIDGE ROAD. NIGHT. {159*, 160*}

Nik reaches over and opens the passenger door. Valerie leans down and peers into the car.

VALERIE: My car's run off the road.

NIK: Get in.

> *Valerie hesitates ... then gets into the ute. He pulls back onto the road. He looks across at her. She is obviously on edge. Her hand rests on the door handle.*

What's your name?
VALERIE: Valerie.

SCENE 163 INT. THE INTERVIEW ROOM – THE POLICE
STATION. NIGHT.   {160*, 161, 162}

(Note: in the finished film the following scene cuts between the police interview room and the Ridge Road.)

NIK: Turns out she lives in one of the houses on the Bay. There's a strip of houses down there. It's out of my way, in the opposite direction almost. Anyway, she doesn't say much. I can tell she doesn't want to talk so I leave it. But I know this short cut and I just don't think.

SCENE 164 INT. NIK'S CAR – THE RIDGE ROAD AND A
TRACK. NIGHT.   {163}

Nik turns off the road along an unsealed track. It happens in a split second. Valerie looks across to Nik, terror in her eyes. He turns to her and is about to say something.

SCENE 165 INT. THE INTERVIEW ROOM – THE POLICE
STATION. NIGHT.   {164}

NIK: And before I can say 'This is the short way' she's gone.
LEON: What are you saying?
{NIK: She jumped out.
LEON: Of a moving car?

> *Nik nods.*

CLAUDIA: We need to hear your answer.
NIK: Yes. She jumped out.

SCENE 166 INT. NIK'S CAR – THE TRACK. NIGHT.

Nik stares at the open door and the empty space.

NIK: [*voice over*] It's dark.

SCENE 167 INT. THE INTERVIEW ROOM – THE POLICE STATION. NIGHT.

NIK: So I can't see her. But I can hear her running through the bush. And I think, 'Jesus, she must be getting cut to shreds', so I yell …}

SCENE 168 EXT. LANTANA BUSHLAND. NIGHT.   {165}

Nik is by his car.

NIK: [*yelling*] Stop … wait …

> *He stops, listens. He can hear her running through the bush. He starts to run after her.*

{SCENE 169 INT. THE INTERVIEW ROOM – THE POLICE STATION. NIGHT.

NIK: I run. It's dark. So I can't see. I trip and fall. That's how I got these cuts on my face.}

SCENE 170 EXT. LANTANA BUSHLAND. NIGHT.   {166*}

Nik's pulling himself out of the lantana, his face cut. He listens. He can hear her crashing through the bush ahead.

NIK: Stop!

> *He listens, but there's nothing, just the sound of breath.*

Vince Colosimo as Nik in *Lantana*. (Photo: Elise Lockwood.)

{SCENE 171 INT. THE INTERVIEW ROOM – THE POLICE STATION. NIGHT.

NIK: And then I don't hear her running any more. But she's close. I can hear her breathing.}

SCENE 172 EXT. LANTANA BUSHLAND. NIGHT.   {166*}

Nik's listening, very still, very careful.
NIK: Lady, don't be afraid. I don't want to hurt you.
      He moves carefully through the lantana, pushing the branches aside.

SCENE 173 INT. THE INTERVIEW ROOM – THE POLICE STATION. NIGHT.   {166*}

NIK: 'Trust me'.

SCENE 174 EXT. LANTANA BUSHLAND. NIGHT.   {166*}

Tight on Valerie – rigid. She turns her head and looks at Nik. There is a moment we think she will give in … and trust. Then …

{SCENE 175 INT. THE INTERVIEW ROOM – THE POLICE STATION. NIGHT.

NIK: But she can't.
      He wipes his eyes.
   And I can understand it. I'm a stranger to her. Why the hell would she trust me? And then she's running again.}

SCENE 176 EXT. LANTANA BUSHLAND. NIGHT.   {166*}

We're with Valerie now. In slow motion. She's running through the darkness. She's bashing her way through the branches. Running and bashing. Running and bashing. Until suddenly there's no ground beneath her. She looks up. It's a release. Then she falls, leaving nothing but black air.

SCENE 177 INT. THE INTERVIEW ROOM – THE POLICE STATION. NIGHT.   {167}

There are tears in Nik's eyes.

NIK: I thought that if I left her alone she'd stop being afraid. So I left her there.

    Nik hesitates, remembering it.

When I got home I saw her shoe on the floor of my car. Jesus, I just wanted to help the woman.

LEON: Why didn't you report it, Nik?

    Nik looks at Leon.

NIK: I just thought she'd be alright, you know? That she'd find her way out of there. And then I heard it on the news … she was missing. And by then … who was going to believe me?

    The three of them are silent, affected.

    Dissolve to:

SCENE 178 INT. VALERIE AND JOHN'S HOUSE. MORNING.   {169}

(Note: in the finished film Scene 168 is outside Valerie and John's house, showing mist on the trees.) John is sitting on the bed. He has the phone to his ear.

JOHN: Thank you for letting me know.

    He places the receiver on the phone. A candle floating in water is burning on the bedside table.

SCENE 179 INT. THE POLICE STATION. MORNING.   {170}

Leon replaces the receiver. He sits at his desk in silence.

SCENE 180 EXT. NIK AND PAULA'S HOUSE. MORNING.
{171}

Paula pulls up in her drive. She gets out of the car. She's been up all night. She looks over to Jane's house.

SCENE 181 INT. JANE'S HOUSE. MORNING.   {172*}

Jane, with the baby in her arms, opens the door to Paula. Paula takes him from her. Her gaze is steely. Jane is unsure. The other kids appear and run and wrap their arms around Paula.

PAULA: Go home, kids.

{JANE: I was going to make them pancakes.

PAULA: Go on.

HANNAH: Where's Dad?}

PAULA: He'll be home soon.

> *Jane stiffens. Hannah and George shuffle out, not sure what's going on.*

JANE: They were so good, Paula. Maybe they can come back later.

PAULA: I don't think so.

> *She starts to go.*

JANE: Paula?

PAULA: He didn't do it.

> *Jane stops. She understands that Paula knows that it was she who phoned the police.*

JANE: How do you know?

PAULA: He told me.

> *Jane is struck by her faith. Paula turns and walks away.*

SCENE 182 EXT. JANE'S HOUSE. MORNING.   {172*}

Jane follows Paula out.

JANE: What could I do?

> *Paula doesn't look back, leaving Jane on the verandah.*

> Paula?

> *Paula doesn't look back.*

SCENE 183 INT. NIK AND PAULA'S HOUSE. MORNING.
                                                      {173}

Paula comes through the back door holding the baby. The sound of early-morning cartoons can be heard on the TV in the other room. She notices it straight away. The dishes have been washed and the table cleared. She hardens.

She moves down the hallway – the clothes and toys have been picked up – and then goes into her bedroom. She sees the made bed and the folded clothes. She feels totally invaded.

SCENE 184 EXT. THE BACKYARD – NIK AND PAULA'S HOUSE. MORNING.   {174}

Paula bursts out of the backdoor and screams over the fence.

PAULA: You've got no right … !

SCENE 185 INT. THE BACK DOOR – JANE'S HOUSE. MORNING.   {174, 179}

Jane is standing at her back door. Rigid. Crying. She can hear Paula screaming at her.

PAULA: [*out of view*] You've got no right!

> *Jane turns and walks through the house to the bedroom where the children slept. Their beds are still unmade. Jane sits on a bed and takes one of the children's teddy bears. She holds it close.*

Daniela Farinacci as Paula in *Lantana*. (Photo: Elise Lockwood.)

(Note: in the finished film this scene is intercut with Scenes 175–178. Paula yells from the fence that she doesn't want Jane anywhere near her kids. Paula returns to her house, and Jane sits on the bed.)

{*Pete comes to the door. He moves to the bed and sits down beside her.*

PETE: It's okay ... [*Almost a question*] We're going to be alright.

> *Jane can't look at him. He looks at the teddy bear.*

Maybe we should have a kid ... It's not too late.

> *She looks at him. There are tears in her eyes.*

JANE: Yeah ... It is, Pete. I'm sorry.

> *Pete holds for a moment. He too is nearly crying.*

I can't go back.}

SCENE 186 EXT. A CLIFF FACE. MORNING.   {180, 181}

Leon and Claudia stand in silence on the edge of the ravine and look out across the lantana-filled valley. They look up at the heavy woosh-woosh of rotor blades. A TV helicopter circles above.

Nik is led back toward a police vehicle after showing them the area where he left Valerie.

Television cars pull up alongside police and rescue vehicles.

Leon looks to see a marked police car pull up. John sits in the front seat. Leon approaches the car as the officer gets out. They exchange a word, then Leon gets into the car with John.

SCENE 187 INT. A POLICE CAR. MORNING.   {182}

Leon and John sit in silence, staring ahead, until finally John speaks.

JOHN: I was home, Leon ...

> *Leon turns his head slowly toward John. The sound of a phone ringing, loud, jarring.*

I didn't pick up the phone.

SCENE 188 INT. VALERIE AND JOHN'S HOUSE. NIGHT.

{183}

Flashback. We hear Valerie's voice in the darkened room.

VALERIE: [*voice over, on the answering machine*] There's lights. There's a car coming. I'll wave it down, John …

> *Pan across to reveal John staring at the phone.*

[*Voice over, on the answering machine*] Wait for me. We'll talk when I get home.

> *John sits still, not moving.*

[*Voice over, on the answering machine*] I love you.

> *He instinctively moves toward the phone then, he hears the click as it is hung up.*

SCENE 189 INT. THE POLICE CAR. MORNING.   {184}

Close on Leon watching John.

JOHN: I thought she would come home.

> *The two men sit in silence, the full weight of what has happened crashing down between them.*

{SCENE 190 EXT. LANTANA BUSHLAND. MORNING.

Tight on Valerie's pale face. Her eyes are open. We can hear the sound of waves. In death she looks composed and unafraid.

Leon stands beside the body. His eye catches the gold band on her finger, her arm hanging by her side. He reaches out and takes her hand, lifting the arm back to her chest.

He steps back as forensic officers move in to lift the body onto a stretcher.}

SCENE 191 EXT. THE CLIFF FACE. MORNING.   {185}

Leon walks back toward his car. Claudia is nearby, talking to a uniformed officer.
CLAUDIA: [*calling over*] Leon …

>*He doesn't respond. He walks to the car and gets inside.*

SCENE 192 INT. LEON'S CAR. MORNING.   {186}

Leon sits for a moment, then removes a tape from his coat pocket. He inserts it in the tape deck and presses 'play'. We hear the static of silent tape space and then:
VALERIE: [*voice over, on tape*] Do you still love him, Sonja?

>*There is a long silence. Leon sits and waits, ready for anything.*

SONJA: [*voice over, on tape*] Yes. I love him.

>*And then it happens. His face cracks, his body slumps, he sobs, his nose and eyes run with tears and snot. He cries – deep and painful.*

SCENE 193 EXT. LEON AND SONJA'S HOUSE. MORNING.
{187}

Claudia pulls the car up. Leon gets out. Claudia watches him a moment, then pulls the car away. He turns and looks at his house. He walks up the path.

SCENE 194 EXT. THE BACKYARD – LEON AND SONJA'S
HOUSE. MORNING.   {188}

The early morning dew sparkles with sunlight. We follow a set of footprints across the lawn, marked in the dew, until we find Sonja sitting in a garden chair.

Her face is drawn, bare of make-up. She looks up at the sound of the back door. Leon is standing there. She watches as he walks across the patio and the lawn until he stands before her.

LEON: I don't want to lose you, Sonja …
SONJA: What … ?
LEON: I don't want to lose you. … I couldn't bear it.

Sonja watches. Music comes over. We pull back until we can see them from above, like watching them from a tree.

Music continues over. (Note: in the finished film Scene 189 is Leon lying alone on his bed.)

SCENE 195 INT. JANE'S HOUSE. DAY.   {190}

Jane is dancing alone, her bare feet pressing into the pile, a glass of wine in her hand.

SCENE 196 EXT. JANE'S HOUSE. DAY.   {191}

Pete sits in his car and watches the house. He starts the engine and drives away.

SCENE 197 EXT. THE BACKYARD – NIK AND PAULA'S HOUSE. DAY.   {194}

(Note: in the finished film Nik walks from his house carrying a child, and lays it down next to Paula on a rug.) {Nik is holding the hose, turning in a slow circle, laughing as the children jump over the rope of water. Paula's sitting on the verandah, sipping a beer and watching them play.}

SCENE 198 EXT. A PARK. DAY.   {193}

(Note: in the finished film Patrick stands outside a cafe in the rain, watching two lovers.) {Patrick is standing in a park. In the distance he can see his lover, walking hand-in-hand with a woman. He watches them a moment, he lets go, then turns and walks away.}

SCENE 199 INT. THE VIETNAMESE RESTAURANT. NIGHT.   {192}

Claudia is eating alone at the table. She looks up at the sound of the door. The mysterious man enters and we see that it is the lonely man Leon ran into, jogging.

He looks over and smiles at Claudia. She smiles back. He approaches the table. We see them talk, then Claudia nods and he sits at the table with her.

SCENE 200 EXT. THE CLIFF FACE. DAY.   {195}

John stands on the edge of the cliff, a wind-torn and lonely figure. He stares down into the ravine where Valerie's body was found.

SCENE 201 INT. LEON AND SONJA'S HOUSE. DAY.   {196}

Leon is lying in his crumpled suit on the bed. His eyes are open. He is silent and numb.

Sonja comes to the bedroom door. She waits a moment, then moves to the bed and lies down beside him. Leon turns over to face her. They look at each other, their faces close.

We see them from above, lying side by side.

SCENE 202 INT. THE DANCE STUDIO. NIGHT.   {197}

The studio is empty except for Sonja and Leon. They are dancing together, tentative, searching, uncertain, but obviously having found a reason to begin again.

Fade.

Credits roll over a cumbia beat.

Kerry Armstrong as Sonja and Anthony LaPaglia as Leon in *Lantana*.
(Photo: Elise Lockwood.)

End Credits

Director RAY LAWRENCE / Producer JAN CHAPMAN / Screenplay ANDREW BOVELL Based on his stageplay *Speaking in Tongues* / Executive Producers RAINER MOCKERT, MIKAEL BORGLUND / Line Producer CATHERINE JARMAN / Director of Photography MANDY WALKER acs / Camera Operator DAVID WILLIAMSON / Production Designer KIM BUDDEE / Costume Designer MARGOT WILSON / Editor KARL SODERSTEN / Sound Designer ANDREW PLAIN / Casting Director SUSIE MAIZELS / U.K. Casting SARAH BEARDSALL / Music PAUL KELLY with SHANE O'MARA, STEVE HADLEY, BRUCE HAYMES, PETER LUSCOMBE

CAST (in order of appearance): Leon ANTHONY LAPAGLIA / Jane RACHAEL BLAKE / Sonja KERRY ARMSTRONG / Steve JON BENNETT / Lisa MELISSA MARTINEZ / Old man in pyjamas OWEN MCKENNA / Sam NICHOLAS COOPER / Dylan MARK DWYER / Drug dealer PUVEN PATHER / Police officers LIONEL TOZER, GLENN SUTER / Claudia LEAH PURCELL / Valerie BARBARA HERSHEY / Young girl NATASHA GUTHRIE / Man at book launch JAMES CULLINGTON / John GEOFFREY RUSH / Patrick PETER PHELPS / Eleanor ASHLEY FITZGERALD / Nik VINCE COLOSIMO / Paula DANIELA FARINACCI / Hannah KEIRA WINGATE / Mystery man RUSSELL DYKSTRA / Harry ANGUS CRIPPS, WILLIAM CRIPPS / Woman dance partner KAY ARMSTRONG / Pete GLENN ROBBINS / Jacob JACOMB BORRA / Jose BEN MORTLEY / Sarah GABRIELLA MASELLI / Newsreader RICHARD MORECROFT / Patrick's lover LANI TUPU / Lover's wife LESLEY HANCOCK / Lover's child ANGUS MCGUIGAN

CREW: First Assistant Director JAMIE CROOKS / Production Manager SUSAN WELLS / Financial Controller CHRISTINE MORAN / Post Production Supervisor GORDON MACPHAIL / Art Director TONY CAMPBELL / Location Manager PETER HARRIS / Costume Supervisor MEL DYKES / Hairdresser JAN "ZIGGY" ZEIGENBEIN / Make-up Artist ROBBIE PICKERING / Continuity KRISTIN VOUMARD / Sound Recordist SYD BUTTERWORTH / Boom Operator GRAHAM MCKINNEY / Second Assistant Director TOM READ / Third Assistant Director GREG COBAIN / On-set Attachment IVY MAK / Focus Puller DAVID ELMES / Clapper Loader MATT WINDON / Video-split Operator GERARD MAHER / Gaffer SHAUN CONWAY / Best Boy STEVE PRICE / Electricians JASON POOLE, BEAU MOULSON, ZAC MURPHY / Key Grip DAVID NICHOLS / Dolly Grip MICK VIVIAN / Assistant Grip ADY ROSE / Rigging Grips GRAEME DEW, ROD SCOTT, JAMES HOPWOOD, MALCOLM BOOTH / Producer's Assistant LEE-ANNE HIGGINS / Production Co-ordinator PAULA JENSEN / Production Secretary TERESA BARKER / Director's Assistant NICHOLAS COPPING / Director's Attachment TONY KRAWITZ / Runner JESSE GIBSON / Art Department Co-ordinator EMMA LAWRENCE / Props Buyers/Set Dressers FAITH ROBINSON, KATE SHARROCK / Standby Props ROBERT 'MOXY' MOXHAM / Additional Art Department Dresser EDMUND LEVINE / Art Department Runner DAVID TIER / Greensman JACK ELLIOTT / Greens Assistants BRUCE RIECK, SUZANNE AUERSWALD, PETER ANNISON / Standby Costume AMANDA IRVING / Costume Assistant NATALIE BRACHER / Costume Cutters MARCIA LIDDEN, JULIE FRANKHAM / Stills Photographer ELISE LOCKWOOD / Publicity MARIA FARMER, MARIA FARMER PUBLIC RELATIONS / Production Notes LEE-ANNE HIGGINS / E.P.K. Cameramen BEN TIERNEY, JESSE GIBSON / Extras Casting AMANDA KNIGHT, MAIZELS PTY LTD / Post Production Accountant GINA HALLAS / Accounts Assistant KRISTIJANA MARIC / Unit Nurse CLAIRE HARRIS / Choreographers MAURICIO ALPIZAR, KIAN SAMADI / Cuban Music Consultant FRANK MADRID / Children's Tutor SARAH MUNRO / Unit Manager

SIMON LUCAS / Unit Assistants PAT LACEY, DAMIAN MACEY, STEWART RIACH, KAREN DOWNES, GREG REFELD / Traffic Control and Security WHO DARES / Additional Location Scouts PHILLIP ROOPE, CHRIS MAYER / Location Attachments JESSE ROBSON, LISA BEEDHAM / Catering CAMERA COOKS, CLAIRE POLLARD / Stunt Co-ordinator LAWRENCE WOODWARD / Safety Supervisor JOHN WALTON / Assistant Stunt Co-ordinator GLENN SUTER / Additional Safety Supervisors LAZARO CIFUENTES / Stunt Performers DAMIEN BRADFORD, LAZARO CIFUENTES, PAUL DOYLE, SAM ELIA, ASHLEY FAIRFIELD, SCOTT GREGORY, TONY LYNCH, LINDA MEGIER, ANDREW OWEN, PUVEN PATHER, TOVE PETTERSEN, BRAD PRAED, GLENN SUTER, ZELIE THOMPSON / tracking vehicle driver GREGORY KING / Stand-in for Anthony LaPaglia DOMINIC MAHONEY / Stand-in for Geoffrey Rush BARRY LORD / Stand-in for Barbara Hershey KATHE THOMAS / Stand-in for Kerry Armstrong VICTORIA COURTENAY / Harry Doubles FRANCESCO STRATI, JAMES WOHL / Dialect Coach for Anthony LaPaglia VICTORIA MIELEWSKA / Editing Facilities KARL MARKS / Assistant Editor DANIEL LEE / Rushes tranfers DIGITAL PICTURES / Laboratory ATLAB AUSTRALIA / Liaison OLIVIER FONTENAY, JAMIE MARSHALL / Negative Matching NEGATIVE CUTTING SERVICES, LEO BAHAS, KERRY AUNGLE, VICKI MCRITCHIE, TONY BEEHAG / Colour Timing ARTHUR CAMBRIDGE / Title Design & Production OPTICAL & GRAPHIC, PETER & AMANDA NEWTON / Dialogue Editor NADA MIKAS / FX Editor MARK WARD / Atmos Editor LINDA MURDOCH / Assistant Editors BRONWYN MURPHY, LIDIA TAMPLENIZZA / Sound attachment PAUL KORBER / Foley Artist JOHN SIMPSON / Sound Editing Facility HUZZAH SOUND / Mixers ROBERT SULLIVAN, ROGER SAVAGE, MARTIN OSWIN / Sound Mixing Facility SOUNDFIRM, SYDNEY / Sound Post Production Facility SPECTRUM FILMS / ADR MICHAEL THOMPSON, ANDY WRIGHT, ROBERT MACKENZIE / LA ADR TODD-AO WEST / Liaison LIZ WRIGHT / Dolby Sound Consultant STEPHEN MURPHY / Film Stock kODAK AUSTRALIA, CATHY CROFT, TIM WAYGOOD / Camera Equipment PANAVISION, PAUL JACKSON / Legal

Representation CLARE MIRABELLO, TRESS COCKS & MADDOX / Insurance TONY LEONARD, JILL DAVIDSON, AON SPECIALTY GROUP / Completion Guarantor ANNI BROWNING, FILM FINANCES, INC. / Post Production Script LESLEY AITKIN / TRAVEL GREG HELMERS, TRAVELTOO / Music PAUL KELLY with SHANE O'MARA, STEVE HADLEY, BRUCE HAYMES, PETER LUSCOMBE / Music Produced by PAUL KELLY, SHANE O'MARA / Music Supervisor CHRISTINE WOODRUFF / Music Recorded at SING SING SOUTH and YIKESVILLE / Music Engineers MATTE VOIGHT, SHANE O'MARA / Assistant Engineer HUGH COUNSELL

Songs
'Descarga Total' written by Isorlando Valle, Ahi-Nama Music/Universal - Musica Unica Publishing, licensed from Universal Music Publishing Pty Ltd, performed by Maraca, courtesy of Ahi-Nama Music and Warner Music France / 'Permiso Que Llego Van Van' written by Juan Formell, Caliente Music Inc/Caliente Music Works LLC, performed by Los Van Van, courtesy of Caliente Music Inc/Havana Caliente LLC / 'Snowdrop' written by Adrian Van De Velde, Origin Music Publishing, licensed courtesy of Festival Music Publishing, performed by Ego featuring Elizabeth Wei, courtesy of Origin Recordings

'Respeta Mi Tambo' written by Pablo Justiz, Ahi-Nama Music/Universal - Musica Unica Publishing, licensed from Universal Music Publishing Pty Ltd, performed by Los Naranjos, courtesy of Ahi-Nama Music

'Opening' written by Lazaro Valdes, Ahi-Nama Music/Universal - Musica Unica Publishing, licensed from Universal Music Publishing Pty Ltd, performed by Bamboleo, courtesy of Ahi-Nama Music

'Te Busco' written by Victor Victor, courtesy of Flamboyan Publishing/ Sony ATV Music Publishing LLC, performed by Celia Cruz, courtesy of RMM Records & Video, Corp

'Que Sabes Tu De Amor' written by Hiran Calvo, performed by Juancyto Martinez, courtesy of Juancyto Martinez

The Producer gratefully acknowledges the assistance of Sergeant Julie Boon, Sergeant Stephen Conroy, Sheridan Australia, Mosman SES, John Highfield, Guerlian, Ericcson, Ryde SES, Bose Australia, Sony Australia, Paul Jackson, Martin Cayzer, George Whaley and all our families

Special thanks to NSW Police Service, Saab Automobiles Australia, Catriona Hughes, Terry Jennings / ABC news footage supplied by Australian Broadcasting Corporation / Soccer footage courtesy of Coast FM – Adelaide / Today Show footage courtesy of Nine Network, Australia / 'Catchphrase' footage courtesy of Southern Star Endemol / 'The Wiggles' audio courtesy of Wiggly Tunes

Shot on location in Sydney, Australia

Panavision / Dolby / Kodak

Developed with assistance from The New South Wales Film and Television Office

International sales Beyond Films / Co-distributed in Australia and New Zealand by Palace Films and Beyond Films MBP

Financed with the assistance of FFC, Australian Film Finance Corporation / All rights reserved. The characters and events depicted in this film are fictitious. Any similarities to actual persons living or dead are purely coincidental.

Copyright in this cinematographic film (including, without limitation, the soundtrack thereof) is protected under the laws of Australia and other countries. Unauthorised copying, duplication or exhibition may result in civil liability and criminal action.

© 2001 MBP Medien AG & MBP KG II, Australian Film Finance Corporation Limited, and Jan Chapman Films Pty Ltd.

About the Author

ANDREW BOVELL writes for the stage and screen. His AWGIE award-winning play *Speaking in Tongues* (Playbox, 1998) has been seen throughout Australia and in London (Derby Playhouse/Hampstead Theatre, 2000), New York (Roundabout Theatre, 2001) and Paris (*La Comédie des Champs-Élysées*, 2002). The screenplay of Lantana was adapted from this play.

Other works for the stage include *Holy Day* (2001), *Shades Of Blue* (1996), *Scenes From A Separation* with Hannie Rayson (1995), *Like Whiskey on the Breath of a Drunk You Love* (1992) and *Distant Lights from Dark Places* (1994). The radio adaptation of this play won the Gold Medal for Drama at the New York Radio and Television Festival and the AWGIE Award for Best Radio Adaptation. Other works include two monologues which featured in the Playbox production of Deidre Rubenstein's show *Confidentially Yours* (1998), an adaptation of *Gulliver's Travels* (1991), *After Dinner* (1988), *The Ballad of Lois Ryan* (1988), *Ship of Fools* (1987 and 1998), *State of Defence* (1987) and *An Ocean Out My Window* (1986). His play *Trash* was produced by ABC Radio in 2000.

With Christos Tsiolkas, Melissa Reeves, Patricia Cornelius and Irine Vela he co-wrote *Who's Afraid of the Working Class* (Melbourne Worker's Theatre 1998) which won the major AWGIE Award in 1999, the Jill Blewitt Award, the Victorian Green Room Award and the Queensland Premier's Award for Drama.

His feature film *Head On*, co-written with Ana Kokkinos and Mira Robertson and based on the Christos Tsiolkas novel, *Loaded,* premiered at the 1998 Cannes Film Festival to critical acclaim.

His work for television includes *The Fisherman's Wake* (*Naked,* ABC 1996), *Lust* (*Seven Deadly Sins,* ABC 1993), *Piccolo Mondo* (*Six Pack,* SBS 1992) and an episode of the telemovie series *Dogwoman* (Simpson Le Mesurier–Network 9, 2000).

Lantana opened the 2001 Sydney Film Festival.

Also by Andrew Bovell

AFTER DINNER

An acutely observed but tender-hearted account of relationships and behaviour set in a suburban pub bistro on a Friday night. The foibles, pain and inner life of the characters emerge as the night proceeds and inhibitions and social restraint are abandoned. 2 Acts—2M, 3W
0 86819 518 9

HOLY DAY

A disquieting story of trust and truth, innocence and faith, set on the white frontier in mid-nineteenth century Australia. A missionary's wife claims that Aborigines have murdered her husband and stolen her child. The only witness to a different story is an Aboriginal woman. Amidst a hostile and misunderstood landscape, this is a chilling mystery about white fear and black resistance. Winner of the 2002 Victorian Premier's Award for Best Stage Play. 2 Acts—4M, 4W
0 86819 646 0

SPEAKING IN TONGUES

A compelling and sophisticated drama exploring betrayal, lust and love between men and women in the 1990s. Winner of the 1998 AWGIE for Best Stage Play and adapted for the screen as *Lantana*. 2 Acts—2M, 2W
0 86819 711 4

SCENES FROM A SEPARATION (with Hannie Rayson)

A fascinating collaboration between two of Australia's most talented writers which presents the male and female perspectives on a marriage. Mathew is forty, a successful publisher whose path is littered with the discarded souls of those who tried to keep up. Nina, his wife of twelve years, is thirty-eight and a journalist. She hasn't worked since the birth of their children, so when Mathew suggests she take on the biography of tycoon, philanthropist and now Australian of the Year Lawrence Clifford, she throws herself into the project with an all-consuming enthusiasm. 2 Parts—3M, 4W
0 86819 476 X

WHO'S AFRAID OF THE WORKING CLASS? (with Patricia Cornelius, Melissa Reeves, Christos Tsiolkas and Irine Vela)

The story of living in an age of social, economic and moral deprivation told through a series of entwined tales about fringe-dwellers who are mostly without work and politically uninterested.
'With intelligence, well-judged humour and the searching qualities of truly memorable theatre, the play peels away political propaganda and notions of correctness to present a candid, difficult, searing portrait of the poor and the marginalised.'
Sydney Morning Herald 1 Act—3M, 3W
Published in MELBORNE STORIES 0 86819629 0

For a full list of our titles, visit our website:

www.currency.com.au

Currency Press
The performing arts publisher
PO Box 2287
Strawberry Hills NSW 2012
Australia

Tel: 61(0)2 9319 5877
Fax: 61(0)2 9319 3649
enquiries@currency.com.au